Specter's

What Not to Do

IRELAND

A Unique Travel Guide

Plan your travel with expert advice and Insider Tips: Travel confidently, Avoid Common Mistakes, and indulge in Art, Culture, History, Food, and nature.

Sarah Brekenridge

Table of Contents

Introduction

The beautiful country of Ireland is well-known for its stunning landscapes, rich history and culture, and the friendly people who occupy the vibrant cities. It's no wonder Ireland is one of the top destinations for people to visit!

Ireland's rugged cliffs of the Wild Atlantic Way, which expands across 1,600 miles along the west coast to the serene lakes in Killarney National Park, can leave any traveler in awe. Even the Cliffs of Moher and Connemara region in Galway can fill you with wonder. It might be exactly as you imagine if you've seen it in films, like Anand Tucker's 2010 film Leap Year or Martin McDonagh's 2022 film The Banshees of Inisherin, but 100 times better in real life. Ireland is simply magical.

The landscapes are one thing that makes Ireland a well-loved place to visit. However, it's also home to numerous historic sites rich with history dating back to the millennia. Ireland has seen everything, from the Vikings and Celts (pronounced kelts) to the warrior clans. Ireland is home to over 30,000 castles and ruins throughout the country, including

- The famous Blarney Castle.

- The Dunluce castle, where you'll be gifted with stunning seaside views.

- The Rock of Cashel that was once a royal site.

- The Bunratty castle is one of the castles that is still mostly intact.

- The Ross castle dates back to the fifteenth century.

You can also visit many filming locations from HBO's Game of Thrones throughout the country if you're a fan of the series!

Visitors love to travel to Ireland to immerse themselves in the rich, unique culture where they can experience traditional music and storytelling while learning more about the country's history and cultural scenes in the various museums and galleries. Ireland has many cultural festivals throughout the year, with St. Patrick's Day being the most significant celebration, particularly in Dublin!

Ireland is famous for its Guinness, but it's also well-loved for its delicious foods. Depending on where you stay, you can expect some delicious, homemade foods and some friendly company to enjoy it with. Ireland's food scene has changed a lot over the years, but you can expect nothing but the best quality in their food. No visit to Ireland will be complete without sampling a pint of their famous stout in one of their cozy pubs!

If that is painting the picture of why you should be starting to plan your trip to Ireland, we are just beginning to plan your grand adventure, whether you are going solo, with a partner, or with your family! Of course, that is the whole thing about wanting to take a trip: Where do you start?

When planning a trip anywhere, even if you're going somewhere in your country, it can feel overwhelming to decide what you want to prioritize. What do you want to see? Are there any festivals that you want to experience? There is so much information available that it can feel like information overload.

As you are starting to think about your trip, you may feel like you need to visit all of the famous sites and cities in Ireland. While Ireland is on the smaller side compared to somewhere like the United Kingdom, please don't feel like you need to see everything in Ireland—especially on the first trip. I will give you a comprehensive guide to all of the beautiful places in Ireland. However, feel empowered to take your journey as your own. Read through each area and decide what is more important based on how long you plan to be in Ireland! You won't see everything, but make sure that as you plan, you're also taking the time to relax where you can.

If you haven't ever been to Ireland and are worried about fitting in, I can tell you that Irish people are some of the kindest souls on the planet. Their love language is to make people feel welcome, from feeding them to chatting. That said, you will learn about how to keep yourself safe, manage your budget, and do other traveling hacks that will make your trip enjoyable.

Throughout this book, you will learn the dos and don'ts of planning your trip to Ireland so you can be fully prepared for it. Everything will be simple and prioritized to minimize your feeling overwhelmed. By the end of this book, you will have a better understanding of Ireland, its culture, and the information you need to choose where you want to go so that you can feel comfortable while traveling the country.

As the old Irish saying goes, May the luck of the Irish lead to the happiest heights.

Chapter 1:

Planning Your Trip to Ireland

T he days when we couldn't step on an airplane to take us elsewhere are long behind us, with many going to many parts of the world to explore. Ireland has been one of those hot spots for people to visit to see the sights in Dublin or escape to the Irish countryside to get a taste of the landscape and the various areas to hike. It's no wonder it's been named one of the top places to visit in Europe, according to Costa (2022), with Ireland earning the title of Best European Travel Destination based on thousands of votes! Let's learn more about the country and some essential planning tips before we dive into each area of the country.

An Overview of Ireland and the Region

Ireland is located west of the United Kingdom on its island, divided into four provinces with 26 counties. These provinces are 1) Munster 2) Connacht 3) Ulster and 4) Leinster

Munster Region

County Clare

The province of Munster is also home to the county of Clare. Clare is famous for its traditional music, but it's here where you will see the sites of the Cliffs of Moher. While in Clare, you can wander The Burren, which will bring you to a stunning rocky landscape famous for its mix of archaeological sites and older farming traditions. If you're there in spring, you'll see wildflowers blooming. This county is also famous for those who enjoy water sports, which you can do in Lough Derg.

County Limerick

Limerick City wasn't painted in the best light in Frank McCourt's Angela's Ashes (McCourt, 1996), which may have deterred people from visiting for a while. In fact, the book is a bit of a "sensitive topic," according to O'Brien (2014). But even though the book paints the picture of McCourt's experience from his family relocating back to the county from New York City during the 1930s, there is much more to see in Limerick than one might think.

Beyond some of the grim backstreets, Limerick's most prominent area is the Crescent, which contains several gorgeous Georgian buildings along an oval-shaped street.

Beyond the quaintness, Limerick is filled with history that can pique anyone's interest, with its famous King John's Castle from the 13th century offering beautiful views of the River Shannon and Limerick's city skyline to St. Mary's Cathedral, famous for its architecture and stained glass windows. Limerick also has the longest footbridge in Ireland, perfect for Instagram posts!

County Cork

County Cork is one of the largest counties in Ireland and home to the oldest yacht club in the world, which was founded in 1720! But despite some of its exciting history, Cork is well-loved and appreciated for its beaches, harbors, islands, and sailing.

Beyond Cork's stunning landscape, it's also home to the famous Blarney stone, where legend has it that if you kiss the stone, you'll be gifted with being eloquent and persuasive. The castle is also something to marvel at if you venture down to this county!

Kerry County

Munster is also home to the county of Kerry, famous among tourists for its picturesque landscape, rugged coastline, and rich cultural heritage. Kerry is many of Ireland's famous landmarks, including the Ring of Kerry, the Dingle Peninsula and the Skellig Islands

Kerry is a perfect spot to visit if you are looking for outdoor activities. It's renowned for its hiking, cycling, and water sports. On the cultural side, Kerry has a fantastic Irish music and dance scene for a fun night out!

County Tipperary

Tipperary is Ireland's largest inland county, surrounded by beautiful countryside. Here, you will find several historic landmarks, such as the Rock of Cashel, a former medieval fortress, and the beautiful Golden Vale Farmlands. Complete with several little towns and villages, Tipperary is perfect for travelers looking to escape the hustle and bustle of the bigger cities and towns.

County Waterford

The county of Waterford is a charming city in the southeast of Ireland, boasting a rich history, beautiful scenery, and a thriving cultural scene. It was once dubbed the "Crystal County" for its production of crystals. Waterford doesn't make them anymore, but visitors love visiting the Waterford Crystal Center to learn more about their former crystal production. Additionally, Waterford has several roots in the medieval era, which tourists love to explore. Some of the attractions to consider visiting are Renigald's Tower and the Viking Triangle.

Aside from the crystal and historical attractions, Waterford is another area where you can see a beautiful coastline and enjoy water sports. In the city, you can enjoy lively music in their pubs and restaurants. If you're looking for things to do that are off the beaten path, consider exploring the ancient holy wells and abbeys in the seaside villages or walking in the Nire Valley.

Leinster Region

Dublin

Dublin is the most well-known city in Ireland as it is the country's largest metropolis and the capital of Ireland as of 1994, taking away its "county" title. Dublin is split into four areas: Dublin City, Fingal, Dun Laoghaire or Rathdown, and South Dublin.

This city is known for its energy, especially if you visit during the week of St. Patrick's Day when a five-day festival runs. However, this is the city where you can see many historical sites, including Dublin Castle, St. Patrick's Cathedral, and Kilmainham Gaol, to get an idea of where Dublin began. Of course, no trip to Dublin would be complete without visiting the Guinness factory and taking a tour to learn about their iconic stout.

County Carlow

The smallest inland county in the province of Leinster area is Carlow. It's not one that many think of visiting, but this little spot is picturesque with its rivers, farmlands, ruins, and small towns surrounded by the Blackstairs Mountains.

If you venture to this area, you will find several historic landmarks, including the ancient dolmen at Brownshill, the ruins of Carlow Castle, and Huntington Castle and its gardens.

In addition to adventuring through many of its monuments and historical spots, Carlow has a fantastic music, theater, and arts scene with several festivals throughout the year. Whether you are interested in the historical side of this area, want to experience nature, or check out the arts, Carlow has something for everyone, and because it's not a well-thought-of place to visit, you'll likely avoid the bustle!

County Kildare

County Kildare borders Dublin and is best known for its horse racing industry. There are plenty of thoroughbreds bred and trained in this county and raced around the Curragh, an unfenced grassy area that spans over 5,000 acres. There are also plenty of gardens to visit, including the famous Japanese gardens. As this area is well known for being one of the largest bog areas, you can learn more about how the Rathangan works to preserve Ireland's boglands and why they are important to Ireland's history at the Bog of Allen Nature Center.

County Kilkenny

Kilkenny has a big personality filled with historical and cultural traits. This county is famous for its Kilkenny Castle and the ancient indigenous Irish sport, hurling, a fast-paced field game.

Just beyond the county's limits, you will find some other charming villages and towns dotted along the River Nore. There are plenty of landscapes to discover that date back to medieval times.

County Wexford

Located in the southeast side of Ireland, Wexford is one area famous for its Viking heritage and the oldest lighthouses in the world on the Hook Peninsula! However, some other things you can check out in this county are visiting the National Heritage Park, which has over 9,000 years of history, and Tintern Abbey, which dates back to around the year 1200! Of course, there are plenty of other houses and gardens to check out, including the Wells House and Gardens, Kilmokea Country Manor Gardens, and the Wexford Garden Trail. In this county, you can also learn about their role during the Great Famine in the mid to late 1840s.

County Laois

Located in the heart of Ireland, Laois has several natural attractions and historical landmarks, making it perfect for a day or two of adventuring. While in this county, it is worth seeing places like the Heywood Gardens, which expands over 50 acres and dates back to the 1700s, the Timahoe Round Tower, which exhibits some of the oldest stonework dating back to the twelfth century, and the ruins of the Rock of Dunamase Celtic fortress that dates back to the ninth century.

County Meath

Go back in time when you go to County Meath to learn more about its history before it became the county it is today. Meath is home to Boyne Valley, a United Nations Educational, Scientific and Cultural Organization (UNESCO) World Heritage site that has some of the more critical archaeological European landscapes, complete with a tomb that is over 5,000 years old!

If you go to Meath, you can hike along the Kells Historic Trail, which dates back to the ninth century. There are plenty of old, historic buildings along the way you can admire. For other outdoor opportunities to enjoy, Meath has plenty of beautiful gardens, including the picturesque Loughcrew Gardens.

County Westmeath

Next to Meath County is the county of Westmeath. Music is the heart of this county, with plenty of concerts and festivals throughout the year. While visiting this area, take some time to explore the various waterways or take a Viking tour! For some tranquility, enjoy some time at the Belvedere House Gardens and Park, which will surely enchant you!

County Longford

The county of Longford has plenty of bustling streets filled with vibrant colors and a beautiful harbor. This is where you can roam through the heritage village, Ardagh, which has the famous St. Patrick's Cathedral, hike in the Cairn Hill Forest, and enjoy a picnic while watching the boats go by on the Royal Canal.

County Offaly

County Offaly is the perfect place for a quick break in your travels if you want a more peaceful atmosphere. You can relax by the River Shannon and watch the fisherman boats drive by or head over to the famous Birr Castle, which has a mix of science, heritage, and culture within its walls where you can see the "Great Telescope" and admire the surrounding gardens. Offaly County is also home to the Tullamore D.E.W. Distillery, which produces the country's famous whiskey!

County Wicklow

Located next to Dublin, the beautiful county of Wicklow is gorgeous and rich in history. This county is home to the Glendalough Monastic site, the most important monastic site in the country, nestled between two lakes and the Powerscourt Waterfall, standing tall at 121 meters!

County Louth

The wee county of Louth is right on the border of Northern Ireland. Though it is teeny compared to the other counties in Ireland, Louth is packed with its historical notes, including St. Joseph's Redemptorist Church, St. Laurence's Gate, and St. Peter's Church, where you see the famous head of St. Oliver Plunkett who was hung for treason in 1681 (if you dare).

Ulster Region

County Cavan

County Cavan isn't high on people's lists to visit unless you're searching for that cozy romantic getaway. There aren't a lot of attractions here, but there are a ton of beautiful lakes, rivers, and forests around it, which is perfect if you and your partner are looking for a great outdoor trip! Some of the things you can do are kayaking or canoeing along the River Erne,

exploring Killykeen Forest Park or wandering through the Dún Na Rí Forest Park, which is rich with history and legend.

County Monaghan

County Monaghan is well-loved for its bountiful lakes, offering a relaxing break from your travels. However, people also love coming to this country to discover the beautiful scenery, complete with rolling hills. In contrast, others will take the time to immerse themselves in the rich history by exploring areas like the historic Clones, the beautiful St. Peter's Tin Church, and the home of the famous poet Patrick Kavaungh.

County Donegal

County Donegal will take your breath away with its tall Derryveagh Mountains surrounding the landscape, offering one of the most majestic scenes in the country. If you're a rock climber, you can spend the day climbing at Malin Head, a cliff overlooking the Atlantic Ocean, or ride along the beach on a horse. Donegal also has some stunning lighthouses, castles, gardens, and some of the best beaches in the country! This is the county to go to if you want to add a different level of excitement to your trip.

Connacht Region

County Galway

Galway might be known for Ed Sheeran's catchy tune, "Galway Girl," but as this region is along the Atlantic Ocean, your breath will be taken away by its coastlines, beaches, and mountains. While in Galway, you can hike along the Diamond Hill, explore the Western and Suckey Valley Ways, or enjoy Irish dancing at the Thatched Cottage. Galway has a vibrant atmosphere perfect for the entire family to explore!

County Sligo

For literature enthusiasts, immerse yourself in W.B. Yeats' history, as Sligo County was the source of inspiration for the former Nobel poet! Here, you can explore his life at the Yeats Building and visit his grave at the Drumcliffe Church. If you're looking for other ancient places to see in Sligo, a trip to Carrowkeel is a must! This is one of the oldest passage tomb cemeteries, with tombs dating from 3200 to 2400 B.C.E.

As for outdoor adventures, you can rock climb with Carraig Climbing, scuba diving, or explore the enchanting Dooney Rock Forest that will give you some breathtaking views of Lough Gill.

County Mayo

The county of Mayo is often on the bucket list of many outdoor enthusiasts and history buffs. In this region, you can visit several historic landmarks, including the Westport House and the Belcarra Eviction Cottage. For adventure and outdoorsy adventures, travelers love riding along the Clew Bay Bike Trail, taking surf lessons, or playing golf at one of the 14 golf courses.

County Leitrim

County Leitrim is a charming and hidden gem in the northern part of Ireland. Here, you can enjoy various activities, including seeing the Glencar Waterfall and exploring Hag's Leap. There are plenty of historical sites in this county, too! Pay a visit to the Manorhamilton Castle and Heritage Center or learn more about ballroom dancing at the Rainbow Ballroom of Romance! You can even board a boat to sail along the Carrick-on-Shannon and experience the longest river in Ireland!

County Roscommon

The county of Roscommon is located somewhat central in the northern part of Ireland and is rich in mining history. You can learn all about life as a miner from former miners and how mining shaped Roscommon.

If you're looking for some fun things to do, check out the Lough Key Forest Activity Park, which features underground tunnels, a bog garden, and some beautiful scenic views as you explore the trails.

The ruins of the Roscommon Castle are another key monument to visit. This castle is from the Norman era in the thirteenth century and was once the home to Hugh O'Connor, the King of Connaught. Although the castle is not fully intact, you can still explore its history while enjoying the surrounding grounds, which include a wildlife conservation area and a bird walk.

Northern Ireland

Did you know that Ireland is two different countries on one island? Not many people do! While Ireland has similar landscapes, it's split into two countries: the Republic of Ireland and Northern Ireland.

The Republic of Ireland (R.O.I.), which we just covered, is part of the European Union, and Northern Ireland is a part of the United Kingdom, meaning that depending on where you go, two different currencies are circulating: the euro (€) in the R.O.I. and the pound (£) in Northern Ireland. This won't impact your travels as there is no physical border between the two countries, but ensure you have your passport documents handy in case you need to show them.

Irish Culture and Cuisine

If you are curious about Ireland's culture and cuisine, there are a few things you should know! In Irish culture, storytelling is one of the most important parts of their culture. For centuries, stories have been passed down through the generations—some in spoken word and others in song. Literature is also highly valued in the country. They have seen many great literary works come from Irish writers such as Jonathan Swift, Oscar Wilde, W.B. Yeats, James Joyce, and Elizabeth Bowen.

In addition to storytelling and literature, dancing is a popular social activity. Traditional Irish Dancing and folk songs have brought people together to enjoy the steps and music that often have a story behind them. Riverdance, in particular, has grown Irish dancing's popularity over the years.

As for the cuisine in Ireland, potato-based foods often come to mind. However, Ireland has a rich history in farming. So sure, you'll find plenty of potato foods while there, but don't forget about their Irish stew and coddle—bonus if you have it with some soda bread!

An Overview of the Best Time to Go

Ireland's weather is temperate, so there isn't necessarily a singular "best" time for traveling there; it all depends on what you are planning or interested in doing, as well as your budget. As you can expect when traveling anywhere in the world, Ireland has its peak season, off-peak season, and shoulder season (which is between the peak and off-peak seasons):

- Off-peak season: October to mid-April

- Shoulder season: mid-April to May

- Peak season: June to September

Ireland's Seasons and Temperatures

Depending on the season you're planning to go to Ireland, here is what to expect in terms of temperatures.

Spring

Ireland's spring season runs from March to the end of May, with the average temperatures between 39.2 °F and 50 °F.

If you travel to Ireland in the spring, you can expect the weather to have a mind of its own. You can expect mild weather for the most part. However, if you're planning your trip to Ireland from March to early April, there may be a few spots of lingering snowy days, whereas in May, the temperature starts to improve.

As for booking flights, the cost is generally lower, especially in April. However, depending on when Easter is, the schools have a two-week break around then, which can cause the cost of accommodations to go up. You can also expect an increase in pricing by May as it's getting closer to the peak season. Crowds-wise, however, it's relatively moderate until the end of May.

Summer

The summer in Ireland runs from June to the end of August, with the average temperatures between 52 °F and 64 °F.

As you can expect, with the warmer temperatures, more people are heading to the beaches to soak up the sun, surf, and rock climb. The summer season is the peak season, so it will be significantly busier at popular attractions, and flights and accommodations will cost more.

Autumn

Autumn runs from September to the end of November in Ireland, with temperatures ranging from about 43 °F to 55 °F.

The weather can vary around this time of the year, ranging between mild and pleasant. There is also the potential for snow by November.

Autumn is when the tourist season starts to wind down, so it's less crowded. Flights are also cheaper and will decrease as the off-peak season sets in. However, depending on where you plan to stay, accommodation prices may remain the same as you would expect during peak season.

Winter

Winter in Ireland is from December to the end of February, with temperatures ranging between 37 °F and 48 °F.

As you might expect, the winter in Ireland can be very wintery. According to O'Hara (2023), Ireland has seen winter storms happen as early as November (but it makes for enjoying plenty of cozy pubs, among other indoor attractions).

Flying to Ireland, as well as accommodations, are more budget-friendly this time of year. You may encounter some crowds, especially if you're going during a

Christmas market or festival. Otherwise, it's pretty calm to see some of the attractions you might have on your bucket list!

Of course, this is just a generic overview. When traveling, one of the best hacks to remember is to check the weather about a week from when you expect to be there to get a better idea of what you should pack! For the expected cooler months, it's a good idea to bring some warm sweaters, waterproof shoes or boots, and a wind and rain-resistant jacket.

Ireland's Year-Round Attractions

Things to Do in the Spring

When spring is in the air in Ireland, the rolling landscapes and farmlands seem to come back to life as it sheds the remainder of winter. The bonus is that it won't be as busy, making your trip quieter. Some of the things you can do in Ireland during the spring include

- visiting a sheep farm
- joining the St. Patrick's Day festivities
- exploring the gardens if you go late spring to early summer
- taking in the landscapes at some of Ireland's hidden gems, such as the Slieve League Cliffs and the Cliffs of Moher
- hiking in the Wicklow Mountains National Park

Things to Do in the Summer

Summer in Ireland is a little more crowded, especially since there are plenty of families going to the country for a holiday. However, with the weather being more favorable, that also lends to its appeal to go if you're looking to enjoy some outdoor attractions without freezing in a cold, damp wind. Of course, seeing the beautiful landscapes, especially the Cliffs of Moher, is a must. However, some of the other things you may want to include

- road trip along the Wild Atlantic Way
- exploring Dublin and the Blarney Castle
- going to the Ring of Kerry
- kayaking or paddle boarding at Killarney Lakes
- ringing the Shandon Bells at the Church of St. Anne in Cork
- exploring world heritage sites
- spending a night at the ring fort
- experiencing a seaweed bath in Slingo County

- bird watching at Saltee Islands
- enjoying a beach day

Things to Do in the Autumn

Ireland's autumn season is when farmers start to harvest their crops, so there is nothing like heading to a local farmer's market to pick up some fresh produce if you're staying at a self-accommodation. With harvest season in full swing, you'll want to check out the St. George's Market in Belfast, Northern Ireland, or the English Market in Cork County. In addition, some of the other top things to do in Ireland during the autumn season include

- joining a fall walking festival in Wicklow County
- going whale watching along the Wild Atlantic Way
- joining Halloween traditions in Derry, Northern Ireland
- taking a scenic ride through the countryside to see the changing leaves
- attending a traditional Irish music festival such as the Cork Folk Festival
- hiking in Connemara National park
- cozying up in an Irish pub after a long day of exploring

Things to Do in the Winter

While many travelers tend to go somewhere tropical in the winter months to soak up the warm sun, winter in Ireland is magical and enchanting, especially around the Christmas season. Some of the top things to do in Ireland during the winter include

- going to the Christmas market in Counties Galway and Cork
- seeing the Northern Lights in County Donegal, Northern Ireland
- watching for wild horses and ponies in the Connemara National Park
- visiting Malahide Castle in Dublin for their Malahide Castle Christmas Experience event
- celebrating the winter solstice at Brú Na Bóinne in County Meath
- checking out the indoor exhibits at the Ulster Museum or the Titanic Belfast museum
- booking a Game of Thrones tour to see the filming sites

Booking Essentials for Ireland

Before looking into your flights and accommodations, consider your budget. It's an obvious rule, but it matters if you're trying to keep your budget minimal! If you're flexible on travel time, you can keep track of prices. Otherwise, it's best to book your flights and accommodations at least six months and no later than three months ahead.

Airports and Flight Research

- Ireland has five international airports to consider when you are looking at flights. They are
- Dublin Airport, located north of Dublin City on the east coast
- Cork Airport, located south of County Cork on the south coast
- Shannon Airport, located north of Limerick on the west coast
- Knock Airport, located in County Mayo in the North West
- Belfast Airport, located in Northern Ireland, west of Belfast City

When looking at flights, it's best to consider the areas you plan to visit in Ireland and what flights are flying into the respective airports. Airlines that fly to the country from North America and Ireland include Aer Lingus, Air Canada, Air Transat, American Airlines, Delta Airlines, Norwegian Airlines, United Airlines, and WestJet.

Now that you know where the major airports are in Ireland, it's time to start looking at flights. Remember, depending on what season you're planning on going will impact the price of the flights; off-peak and shoulder seasons tend to have more budget-friendly pricing compared to peak season. Google is an excellent option to check as you can filter the prices and dates using their "date grid" and track the prices. Additionally, flying mid-week is also more cost-effective as opposed to flying to Ireland on a Friday, Saturday, or Sunday.

Accommodations

Depending on what season you're planning to go to Ireland, the prices for accommodations will vary. Again, knowing what season you want to go and being flexible about going during off-peak and shoulder season can help keep some more money in your pocket. From there, it's what kind of accommodation you want to consider. Bed and breakfasts are some of the more common accommodations to stay at. You'll likely enjoy a full Irish breakfast every morning and have a pleasant atmosphere with the hosts. If you're looking for an outdoor excursion, there are camping and glamping sites available. You can even stay in a lighthouse! There are also cottage accommodations you can look into, as well as Airbnbs and hotels. To give you a better idea of pricing, consider how much you'd be willing to spend per night:

- If you are camping or glamping, it can be between €10 and €15 per night.

- If you are staying at a bed and breakfast, it can be between €30 and €50 per night.
- If you are staying in a hotel, it can range between €50 and €60 per night.
- If you are staying at a cottage, it can range between €80 and €100 per night.
- If you are planning to rent an Airbnb, the average price per night is around €168 (but this can vary based on where the accommodation is and the season).

When looking at your accommodations, consider where you want to stay and how you plan to get around Ireland. If you're renting a car, consider if your accommodation has parking available. If you're not renting a car, consider how close you are to the nearest bus or train station. The train networks in Ireland are the Irish Rail in the Republic of Ireland and the Translink in Northern Ireland. In addition to transportation and parking, you will also want to consider what amenities are available, such as whether breakfast is included.

Activities and Tours

After you book your flights and accommodations, don't forget about booking the activities and tours you want to do ahead of time to ensure they aren't all booked up or sold out. Most bookings can be done about a week to up to three days before. Anything after that is when you are at a higher risk of being unable to visit a museum or take a tour.

Most things can be booked online. When we look at the different things you should do and experience in the other parts of Ireland, I'll give you more information on how to book and the pricing. However, if you want to use a travel operator to secure some of your tours, the top companies are Collette, Contiki, Overland Ireland, Trafalgar, Globus, Rabbie's Small Group Tours, Irish Experience Tours, On The Go Tours, Back-Roads Touring, Tenon Tours, and Tours of Distinction.

Planning Your Trip

The Right Way to Pack

It's really easy to overpack for a trip! However, recent hacks are popping up everywhere. But before we get into the hacks of packing, some of the essential clothes you'll need for Ireland include

- lightweight layers (a layer with smart wool is handy)
- warm sweater
- jeans or leggings
- shorts (if you're going in the summer)
- a swimsuit (if you're going in the summer)

- a wind and rain-resistant jacket or shell
- good walking shoes and hiking boots
- a hat
- scarf and gloves (if you're going in during the cooler seasons)
- insulated boots (if you're going in the winter)
- down jacket (if you're going in the winter)
- windproof umbrella

Okay, now that you have the basics, let's talk about trying to pack as minimally as possible because that is something many people try to do. First, compression packing cubes should be your best friend. These come in different sizes and can help to decrease the amount of space and bulk in your luggage. You can find them on Amazon. Otherwise, Ziplock bags also do wonders for this purpose!

When packing your clothes, organize your outfits based on the day. Using a notepad or something on your phone is handy to give you a visual, especially if you are moving from one place to the next every day or every couple of days. Having the visual will allow you to see where you can mix and match clothing items per day.

After you have your outfits sorted, it's time to pack them into your packing cubes or Ziplock bags. Break the outfits up into three different packing cubes that will correspond with the days you plan to wear the items. So, for example, in one packing cube, you'll put the first three days, and in the second bag will be the remainder of your outfits. Label the compression bags as well so you know what you are looking for and to help keep your luggage somewhat packed. In the third compression bag, you may pack miscellaneous items you're not sure you'll need, such as a swimsuit, scarf, and gloves. You may also want to pack an empty compression bag for dirty items until you have access to laundry (or pack some laundry sheets if you won't have access to a washing machine).

As for toiletries, try to keep them minimal! You don't need full-size bottles of shampoo and conditioner. Put them into travel-size containers, as they will save you space in your bag! Things like sunscreen can be bought while you're there if you need it, as well. It's also a good idea to bring a smaller backpack for your daily outings.

Travel Insurance

The age-old question of whether you should invest in travel insurance or not when you're planning a trip is a big one. Travel insurance is not a requirement, but it does give you peace of mind if something were to come up or happen that would prevent you from going to Ireland. It can also help you avoid paying for medical expenses out of your pocket if a medical issue were to arise on your trip.

As for choosing your travel insurance carrier, there are plenty on the market. However, websites such as InsureMyTrip.Com will let you compare the prices between different carriers. What you should be looking for when shopping for travel insurance is - trip cancellation coverage, trip delay coverage, trip interruption coverage, medical expenses, emergency-evacuation benefits, and baggage loss coverage.

Currency Exchange and Money-Saving Hacks

As Ireland does not take dollars, it's best to use a mix of currency and card payments. Keep in mind that Ireland is split into two countries, so if you're in the Republic of Ireland, you'll need euros, and if you're in Northern Ireland, you will need pounds. Therefore, if you travel between the two, you will need a mix of both currencies to bring cash.

As for cards, Ireland accepts most major credit cards except American Express, Discovery, Diners Club International, and J.C.B.

If you need to exchange currency, you will need to find a currency exchange outlet. It's better to do this before you travel, but if you forget, the airports will have them; however, that should be your last resort because it tends to be more expensive. Beyond the airport, Ireland has plenty of currency exchange companies you can get currency from, but again, it can be pricey! Therefore, if you need to exchange currency in Ireland, go to an ATM, as the fees are less expensive and generally safe and reliable. If you exchange ahead of time, it's good to bring at least €200 and then pay the rest by card. If you're spending a few days in Northern Ireland, get at least £200.

As for money-saving hacks, here are something to look into that may help make your planning easier while saving some money in the process:

- Book an Ireland bed and breakfast adventure through Aer Lingus: Aer Lingus offers tour packages up to nine nights with your choice of bed and breakfast accommodations. It's a self-drive tour, but you will get
  - o a round-trip economy class airfare flying into Dublin or Shannon.
  - o a manual transmission rental car for your trip (you can upgrade to automatic).
  - o to stay at the Hotel Woodstock in County Clare (or something similar) for one night
  - o five, six, seven, or eight nights at a bed and breakfast of your choice throughout the country.

-     o   daily breakfast.
- Visit museums: Most museums throughout the country are free, which is a great way to save money!
- Buy a Heritage Card: Heritage cards are about €40 for adults or €30 for seniors 60 and up. This card will give you access to over 65 attractions in Ireland, except Muckross Traditional Farms. If you're traveling with children between 12 and 18, this card is €10.
- Stay in a hostel: If you're a traveler who is 30 and under, hostel accommodations are usually a top option because they're cheap. Dublin has a well-rated one called the Generator, which costs roughly €22.68 per night. If you're looking for a hostel, do your research and make sure that they are clean and safe as well as budget-friendly.
- Eat in: If you're staying in self-catering accommodation, consider making some of your meals at your home away from home instead of eating out every day. Groceries tend to be a little on the cheaper side in Ireland, and it saves money on restaurant prices.

What to Avoid When Planning a Trip to Ireland

Whether or not you have planned a trip before, you will know that it comes with plenty of indecisions and obstacles. Going to a country like Ireland can feel overwhelming with the number of things to see and do in such a small country. Knowing some of these common mistakes should help you make your planning a little more seamless now so that you can see as much of the country as you can in whatever amount of time you will be there.

Don't Try to Squeeze Too Much into a Short Trip

Ireland may look small on the map, but even though it's a small country, there is a lot to cover around the island! So, don't think you can cover all of the regions, their counties, and their tiny towns and villages if you're only going to be there for a short trip. It's not going to be possible to see everything, so instead of trying to see everything you "think" you should see, choose what your must-see locations are and make those a priority. However, be mindful of where these destinations are so you're not driving all over the place trying to get from one place to the next. Pick three or four counties nearby and explore what they have.

Don't Spend Most of Your Time in Dublin

Dublin is a lively place in Ireland; that should come as no surprise given that it's the country's capital! But don't spend your entire vacation there; take the odd mini-day trips to nearby counties and towns. Sure, check out Dublin if you want, but it's an expensive city for accommodations, and it's pretty busy! So, if you want to experience the rolling hills and the stunning scenery, try staying in a county along the coasts.

Don't Forget the Bed and Breakfasts

If there is one thing that Ireland is well-known for, it's their welcoming bed and breakfasts! This is especially beneficial if you're traveling with kids, as trying to book a hotel with adjoining rooms can take time and effort to find. Plus, you'll feel like a part of the family as most bed and breakfasts are family-owned, and the locals likely will have intel on some of the hidden gems you might not even know about!

Don't Only Stay in The Republic of Ireland

For some strange reason, there is an invisible line in the sand where people think that because Northern Ireland is not necessarily part of the entire island, it must be dangerous. Was it because of the troubles that happened over 20 years ago? The country has been peaceful ever since, and you might miss the charming towns in Northern Ireland's six regions if you don't go, especially if you want to learn more about the Titanic!

Don't Be Afraid to Drive in Ireland

Yes, Ireland drives on the opposite side of the road, which is intimidating for US and Canadian drivers, but don't be afraid to drive in Ireland, or else you will limit yourself to day trips from Dublin and other major cities in the country. By renting a car, you will see much more of Ireland and the gorgeous landscapes between your destinations.

Don't Spend Money on an International Cell Phone Package

While most cell phone services offer international roaming, it can be pricey when you add it up per day. Chances are, you won't need to call back home. What you can do instead is get an e-SIM or SIM card for your phone that will give you unlimited data for the amount of time you will be there. HolaFly is a popular option for an e-SIM company, and it is effortless to set up!

Don't Forget to Plan Your Budget in Advance

When traveling to a country like Ireland, you should plan your budget because things will add up quickly. Of course, the more significant expenses start with the flights, hotels, and car rentals. From there, you'll want to plan a daily budget for activities and food. You can save money if you go grocery shopping because you've chosen a self-catering accommodation and you're exploring free attractions.

Don't ignore unpredictable weather.

Ireland's weather can be unpredictable, with rain a common occurrence. Be prepared for varying weather conditions by packing layers, waterproof clothing, and sturdy shoes suitable for walking in potentially wet terrain.

Don't overlook local festivals and events.

Check for local events, festivals, and holidays happening during your visit. Participating in or avoiding these events, depending on your preferences, can enhance your travel experience and help you plan accordingly.

Ireland has plenty of things to see and do for travelers looking for a mix of history, culture, natural beauty, outdoor activities, and cozy settings. From the bustling city of Dublin to the tranquil countryside with its rolling hills, each region in Ireland has a unique character and charm worth exploring. But of course, to cover all of that will take more than one trip! So, if you've never been or are planning a return trip, use the tricks and tips in this chapter to help you research and prepare your itinerary in advance to make the most of your trip!

In the next chapter, we will be exploring the tips and tricks to traveling around Ireland and some of the safety etiquette to ensure your trip is enjoyable and stress-free.

Chapter 2:

Tips and Tricks to Explore Ireland

Ireland has many trivial facts, but many people are surprised by some of the country's unusual tidbits!

Fun Facts about Ireland

St. Patrick Is Not Irish!

Let's start with St. Patrick. St Patrick's Day is famous around the globe, with many countries celebrating with green beer on the iconic March 17 date, which is supposedly the day St. Patrick died. But did you know that St. Patrick wasn't Irish?

St. Patrick was born in Great Britain, formerly Britannia, around the year 386, which means he was not Irish. His family was wealthy, and according to the History.com Editors (2023), St. Patrick was taken hostage when a group of Irish raiders were "attacking his family's estate." These Irish raiders took St. Patrick from his family and brought him to Ireland.

St. Patrick escaped his captors six years later, and according to some of his writing, he said a voice that he believed was God's told him it was time to leave the country. When he returned to Britain, St. Patrick had another dream where an angel told him to return to Ireland "as a missionary." (History.com Editors, 2023a). St. Patrick entered the church and underwent 15 years of religious studies, and then was eventually ordained as a priest and returned to Ireland.

When St. Patrick returned to Ireland, he integrated Irish culture into his Christianity lessons. For example, St. Patrick incorporated bonfires to "celebrate Easter," as the Irish used fire to "honor their gods" (History.com Editors, 2023a).

So, while many believe St. Patrick is famous for removing snakes from the island, it is all a myth. It should come as no surprise since Irish culture loves to tell oral stories, and St. Patrick's life became embellished as the tales were passed down among generations. However, while the stories of St. Patrick's life have become widely exaggerated over the years, it shows how much the Irish love to spin exciting stories to remember their history.

St. Valentine's Remains Are in Dublin

It might sound morbid, but the remains of St. Valentine are in the Whitefriar Street Church in Dublin. Couples visit the shrine to pray to this saint and ask him to watch over them. There are a few myths surrounding St. Valentine and his life. But in short, it's believed he was beheaded on February 14 in Rome after trying to convert Emperor Claudius II to the Christian faith. So, how does St. Valentine relate to Ireland?

Father John Spratt was an Irish Carmelite priest, and he visited Rome in 1835. Having impressed Pope Gregory XVI, St. Valentine's remains were exhumed from the Roman catacombs for Father Spratt to bring back to Dublin. According to Daly (2022), St. Valentine's remains arrived in Dublin on November 10, 1836, and thousands of people followed the procession of St. Valentine as his remains made their way to Whitefriar Street Church. There was much interest in St. Valentine for the next 35 years until Father Spratt died in 1871. St. Valentine's remains were eventually stored and forgotten until a major renovation to expand the church began in the 1950s. As a result of the discovery, a shrine was implemented and is still there today in a side altar where couples visit to pray for their love or to find love; however, on Valentine's Day, the shrine is moved to the high altar as part of the feast-day for this saint.

Ireland Is Where Halloween Originated

Halloween is a kid's favorite holiday because it's the day they can get free candy! But did you know this iconic holiday originated in Ireland? Not many do!

Halloween is traced back to the early days of Paganism in Ireland over 2,000 years ago. This was when Irish people celebrated the festival of Samhain, which marks the end of summer, according to Lang (2018). During ancient times, the Celts would burn hearth fires until the fire died while families harvested. When the harvest was completed, the celebrations would continue with the Druid priests, who used a wheel to light a community fire as it represented the sun. The festival was a symbol of celebrating death and rebirth.

By the year 609, Pope Boniface IV declared the day before Halloween to be called All Saints' Day. However, this day was moved by Pope Gregory III to after Halloween (so November 1) to correspond with when Samhain would have been held in the ancient Celtic era. This day was a celebration of those saints and martyrs who died.

The practice and rituals changed over the centuries, eventually morphing into what we know Halloween to be today with the "Pagan-turned-Christian practices of dressing up in costume, playing pranks and handing out offerings" have shifted, even if people don't believe in ghosts or saints (Lang, 2018). However, the trick-or-treating aspect we know well was used in the ancient Irish and Scottish times that led up to Samhain. The Irish were the ones who dressed up in costumes, went door-to-door, sang songs to the dead, and were rewarded with cake. So, while your kids don't need to pull tricks to get candy, it is an exciting piece of the history of spooky season!

The Longest Coast in the World Is the Wild Atlantic Way

The Wild Atlantic way along the Irish West coast is the longest western seaboard in the world. It stretches across 1,533 miles from the beautiful seaside town of Kinsale, in County Cork in the south, to the Inishowen Peninsula in County Donegal in the north.

Dublin Is Home to the Oldest Pub in Ireland

The Brazen Head is Dublin's oldest pub in Ireland. It opened in 1198, and though it's unknown what part of the original eleventh-century coach house is still a part of the pub today, there is enough history sprinkled throughout.

As you enjoy a pint, check out the historic prints and scrolls on the walls. If you're there in the summer, they have a wonderful cobblestone courtyard where you can enjoy pints alongside traditional dishes if you want a formal dining experience.

With those quick, fun, and weird facts in mind, let's discuss some tips and tricks for exploring Ireland.

Getting Around Ireland

Driving is one of the better options for getting around Ireland because it will allow you to see much more of the landscape. But it's understandable if driving a manual car (though you can book a car with an automatic transmission) coupled with driving on the opposite side of the road is a hard no for you. So, if driving is not going to be a thing, don't worry; there are other ways to get around the island.

By Bus

If you're looking for a leisurely way to travel around the country and connect with fellow Irish travelers, the bus and coach tours are the way to go! You can experience the island from the comfort of your seat and not worry about navigating your way around!

There are two primary providers for getting around Ireland. In the Republic of Ireland, the bus and coach services available are through Bus Éireann and, in Northern Ireland, Translink. There are other smaller providers you can also look into, including tour companies, if you have an itinerary in mind, such as golfing or seeing different castles.

In Northern Ireland, there is an iLink smartcard that will give you unlimited bus and rail travel in specific zones, which will save you money. There is also a Leap card for the Republic of Ireland transportation that you can use if you are in the following cities and counties: Dublin, Cork, Galway, Limerick, Waterford, Sligo, and Athlone.

The Leap card can also be used for unlimited travel in Dublin. See the "By Trams" section for more information.

By Train

Ireland has two rail networks that run through the country. Irish Rail serves the Republic of Ireland, while Translink runs in Northern Ireland, with Dublin and Belfast being the main hubs. If you're looking to travel between Belfast and Dublin, the Enterprise Train is the fast and efficient way to do this. Even so, train rides take 2.5 hours at most to get between destinations, making them more efficient than the bus.

If you use the Irish Rail train network, you need to prebook your tickets, but they can be bought at the station or online. You can also use a Leap Card if you are traveling within Dublin. Of course, all information, including buying your tickets, can be found on their respective websites.

By Taxis or Ubers

Taxis are another great way to get around Ireland, and it's a chance to chat with a friendly local who likely knows a lot of good places you want to check out while on your travels. Taxis are around most major cities but might be harder to find in small towns or rural areas. Your best bet is to ask locals if there is a taxi service they recommend. Ubers are also an option. However, the service can only be offered by a registered taxi driver.

If you want to prebook a taxi service, you can use the FreeNow app. Taxis can be booked up to four days in advance. However, you can also use the app to book a taxi service when needed. The FreeNow app can only be used in Cork, Galway, Dublin, Limerick, and Waterford.

Some taxi services also offer tour services where your driver will give you a tour of the city or region you're visiting.

One last note in terms of taxi fares: They are metered except for in Hackney. If you are taking a taxi in Hackney, you will need to agree on a fare with your driver before you get going.

By Bicycle

Given the stunning landscape of Ireland, cycling around it is one of the greatest ways to experience its beauty. There are plenty of routes to serve varying levels if you're looking for a more casual sightseeing experience. However, you can also join a guided bike tour, such as along the Wild Atlantic Way.

There are plenty of bicycle shops you can rent from, and the fees are relatively reasonable. The prices generally include a pump, puncture repair kit, lock, mudguards, and a carrier. You will want to ask about bike helmets to see if they are included in the rental fee, which can vary per shop.

By Trams

Dublin's tram system is called Luas, which is Gaelic (an Irish language) for "speed." Two lines service Central Dublin and some of the residential areas in the south and southwest of Dublin. Trams run from 1) 5:30 a.m. to 12:30 a.m. Monday to Friday, 2) 6:30 a.m. to 12:30 a.m. on Saturdays and 3) 7:30 a.m. to 12 a.m. on Sundays

Tickets can be purchased from the machine at each stop. It's not overly expensive, but if you're going to be in Dublin for a few days, it might be worth it to save paying the fare each time and use a Leap Visitor Card that will give you unlimited travel throughout the period you pay for. You can also use this card on Dublin City Bus services and the Commuter Rail. The options available for the Leap Visitor Card are One day: €8, Three days: €16, and Seven days: €32.

The period will begin when you tap your card for the first time. There are over 2,000 places in Dublin you can buy a leap card from, so check out their website for the closest location to your accommodation.

Renting a Car

If you want to rent a car in Ireland because you don't have a specific schedule you are sticking to or wish to have the ease of getting around the country, you need to be at least 25 years old with a valid driving license. You can rent a car from Europcar, Enterprise, Sixt, Hertz, or Ireland's local spot, Dooley. However, if you're trying to save money on your car rental, use Discover Cars, as this website will help you find the best price. However, for conversion's sake, car rentals are between \$25 to \$40 USD per day, depending on the type of car you rent. Additionally, you can expect the car rental price to be higher if you're looking to rent a car with an automatic transmission.

In terms of filling up on gas, Ireland fills up by the liter versus the gallon, so if you have a car that runs on diesel, it will be somewhat cheaper to fill up.

Staying Safe in Ireland

While Ireland is known for its friendly atmosphere, you should refrain from throwing caution to the wind and not make your safety a priority, which can put a damper on your travels.

Personal Safety

Ireland's crime rate is low for the most part, but you should still be aware of your surroundings to keep yourself and your family safe while traveling through the country. This means that you are keeping your belongings in eyesight (unless you're taking a coach bus and need to store luggage under the bus and ensure petty criminals aren't going to pickpocket from your backpack. Obviously, this is common sense, but if you can try to blend in rather than make yourself stand out, the safer you'll be!

Emergency and Assistance

If you are in a situation where you require emergency services (the police (called Garda Síochána), ambulance, Coast Guard, or the fire brigade), the number to call is 112 or 999. It's also a good idea to buy travel insurance that will cover medical costs if you need to see a doctor while in Ireland.

The U.S. Embassy is located in Dublin at 42 Elgin Road, Ballsbridge. You can also call them for an emergency at +353 1 668 8777. You can also find the embassy in Northern Ireland at 223 Stranmillis Road in Belfast. Their phone number is +44 28 9038 6100.

What NOT to Do – Safety

Don't Go to the Edge of the Cliffs

I know it's tempting to want to go to the edge of the cliffs to take an epic selfie, but it's just not safe! Yes, there aren't fences to prevent you from going near it, but it doesn't mean it's an invitation to test your fate. According to O'Connell (2020), 68 people died from falling off of the edge at the Cliffs of Moher between 1993 and

2019, which is a tragic statistic. So, please don't go near the edge, as tempting as it might be. I promise you will get plenty of great photos from a safe distance.

Don't Forget to Be Aware of Your Surroundings

While Ireland's crime rate is relatively low, it's still good to be mindful of your surroundings, especially when visiting bigger cities like Dublin or Belfast. If something doesn't seem right, trust your gut and walk away.

Don't Leave Valuables and Luggage Visible in Your Car

If you're renting a car and are parking in a public space, ensure any valuables and luggage are out of sight. Likewise, don't leave luggage attached to your roof rack.

Don't Drive on the Right Side of the Road

While we drive on the right side of the road in the U.S., remember that it is the opposite in Ireland! Likewise, their driver's side is on the right side instead of the left.

While on the topic of driving, there is also a big etiquette while on the road, and that is to acknowledge other drivers, such as a quick greeting to a passing car.

Interacting With the Irish

Irish people are a chatty bunch, even to a perfect stranger on the street. For them, making small talk is important as it's seen as a polite way to interact with one another. The Irish are also very big on using "please" and "thank you," so don't forget these important phrases wherever you go! For example, instead of saying, "I'll have a pint of Guinness," say, "I'll have a pint of Guinness, please." Likewise, if someone were to open a door for you, say, "Thank you." This is common sense, but sometimes we forget our manners, even at home!

While walking around the towns and cities in Ireland, you'll come across many locals. It's customary to nod and smile as a way of saying "good day" or saying hello to them. If you recall earlier, this is also a way the Irish interact with one another when they drive by each other, even if they're perfect strangers.

As you may know, pub culture is big in Ireland, but it isn't only about having a few pints. Pubs are the places where locals socialize with one another or meet up with friends. So, if you end up in a conversation with some others in the pub, chances are you'll be going home with some new friends! That said, also be mindful of if you're being too loud. Irish people tend to speak in softer tones (not just inside pubs and restaurants but elsewhere, too).

Interacting with the Irish is not a complicated thing, and it's going to make your trip so much more fun! When you can be open, friendly, and respectful to the locals, you'll discover how warm Ireland can be to non-locals.

Ireland's Sacred and Historical Sites

Historical sites in any country are always something to admire and appreciate, especially in countries like Ireland, where the historical side of it is centuries old!

When you go to visit the sacred and historical sites, remember to appreciate their value. Many areas in Ireland are recognized by UNESCO, which makes them an important part of Ireland's history. We're so lucky to be able to experience these spots and share that experience with others, but remember that while it might be a pasture with miles of rolling hills or ruins of a castle, let the value sink in.

As you wander through the various historical places on your itinerary, remember to verify about photography. It can be tempting to take photos of everything, but some places may have policies that prevent you from taking photos. In the worst case, if you need clarification and there is a visitor's center, ask them.

Lastly, remember that you are a visitor to Ireland. Treat the places you are visiting as you would going to a friend's house. This will make your trip more enjoyable for yourself and the fellow travelers you come across.

What NOT to do in Ireland

There are many things for you to do in Ireland. But you want your trip to be memorable as you dive into their culture and experience their rich history. This section will cover everything you should avoid while in Ireland.

Don't Call St. Patrick's Day "St. Patty's Day"

Back home, we may call St. Patrick's Day "St. Patty's Day," but that's not something the Irish will ever refer to that day as. It will annoy every Irish person who hears you say, "Happy St. Patty's Day!" you'll make yourself stand out like an American or Canadian tourist—so don't do it.

Don't Make Potato Jokes

While the Irish are known for their quick wit and sarcastic jokes, joking about potatoes is something you shouldn't do. When the Great Famine hit Ireland during the 1800s, it was a dark time with many deaths due to the lack of food and produce; many died on their way to immigrating elsewhere (mainly America, Canada, and Australia) or faced hardship upon arrival.

Don't Forget to Buy a Round

If someone buys you a round in a pub, it's common courtesy to do the same, even if you're a tourist! You can, of course, politely decline a round by communicating that you're buying your drinks, especially since buying rounds can become pricey!

Don't Talk About Leprechauns

The locals aren't fascinated with the idea of a leprechaun like the rest of the world might be. While they are a part of Ireland's mythology and legends, Irish people don't care for them all that much, nor do they search for these mythical creatures. However, if you are curious about them, you can visit the National Leprechaun Museum in Dublin.

Don't Tip in Pubs

Tipping isn't a big thing in Ireland, so don't feel obligated to leave a tip. However, if you want to show gratitude, you can leave enough to cover the cost of a drink (somewhere between €4 and €6) and say, "and one for yourself."

Don't Forget to Pack Good Walking Shoes

Many of the ancient monuments and ruins in Ireland are a bit of a hike, so you will want to make sure you are wearing good walking shoes or hiking boots to get to them. It's a good idea to make sure your shoes are suitable for adverse weather or terrain, especially since some of the footpaths can be impacted by rainy weather.

Don't Assume Public Transport Will Get You Everywhere

While the major cities have public transportation systems to get you from different points, don't rely on public transportation to get you everywhere, especially in remote rural towns. You'll want to investigate other ways to get to different spots if you are not renting a car. The locals will be accommodating in this case!

Don't Be Afraid to Go Off the Beaten Path

There are plenty of attractions that are recommended for tourists to go to, but don't be afraid to explore other parts of Ireland that may not be top on the "to visit" lists. You will never know what you will find!

Ireland is a country filled with a unique and fascinating history, from St. Patrick's true story to the origins of Halloween. Although those are just some of the tidbits few know about, this chapter has helped to guide you on exploring Ireland and doing it safely while interacting with the Irish people. In the next chapter, we will wander through the streets of Dublin to learn more about this famous city and, of course, what you should avoid doing while there.

Chapter 3:

Dublin—Dos and Don'ts

As the capital of Ireland, Dublin's thriving city attracts thousands to its streets yearly. But what is Dublin known for? Well, one of the things Dublin is famous for is that it's a progressive and friendly city. It was voted the "sixth friendliest city in the world," according to Corcoran (2020). You will see for yourself if you converse in a pub! However, Dublin's progressiveness comes forward when it comes to culture and inclusivity, and Dublin has one of the best pride events every June!

Dublin is also one of the six cities to receive a "City of Literature" status from UNESCO (Corcoran, 2020). Dublin's famous authors Yeats, Beckett, Shaw, and Heaney are all Nobel prize winners.

Of course, you can't forget the vibrant pub culture, and Dublin is home to over 1,000 pubs! You can't go anywhere without walking by one as they are the center of the social life in Dublin!

Although Dublin is one of the bigger cities and busier than some of the smaller towns, it's definitely a place to spend at least two days in Ireland because of its rich culture. Let's explore some of the things to do and experience in Dublin.

What to DO in Dublin

Although Dublin is the Republic of Ireland's capital, it's as friendly as walking into a pub in a smaller town. However, this gorgeous and vibrant city has a river running through it, colorful art throughout its streets and alleys, and a rich history. Let's look at several things you could do if you are planning to visit Dublin.

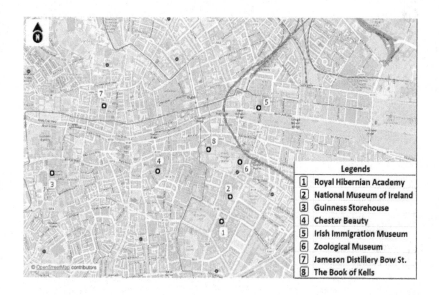

Legends

1. Royal Hibernian Academy
2. National Museum of Ireland
3. Guinness Storehouse
4. Chester Beauty
5. Irish Immigration Museum
6. Zoological Museum
7. Jameson Distillery Bow St.
8. The Book of Kells

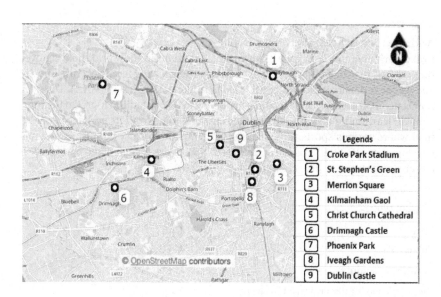

Legends

1. Croke Park Stadium
2. St. Stephen's Green
3. Merrion Square
4. Kilmainham Gaol
5. Christ Church Cathedral
6. Drimnagh Castle
7. Phoenix Park
8. Iveagh Gardens
9. Dublin Castle

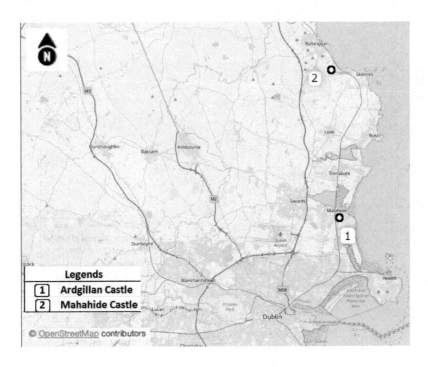

Legends
| 1 | Ardgillan Castle |
| 2 | Mahahide Castle |

© OpenStreetMap contributors

Croke Park Stadium

Address: Jones' Rd, Drumcondra, Dublin 3

Croke Park Stadium is Europe's third largest stadium in the world, holding over 82,000 fans to watch and cheer over their favorite sporting teams playing hurling and Gaelic football, organized by the Gaelic Athletic Association (GAA). Discover how central Croke Park is in Ireland's history by taking a stadium tour. On the tour, you will learn more about how the stadium came to be from its earlier years as a field where various sports took place and its intricate history with the stadium's development after the land was purchased. Sports are a significant part of Irish culture, so if you're a sports fan, this tour is for you.

Ticket type	Cost of admission
Adults	€ 16
Children	€ 11
Students/seniors	€ 13
Family (two adults and two children)	€ 43
Family (two adults and three children)	€ 45

For tour dates and times, you will need to see their website to see what is available when you select your ticket type.

St. Stephen's Green Park

Address: St Stephen's Green Square, in Dublin 2

The historical park of St. Stephen's Green Park is an excellent spot to take a break in your day, providing a calming green space in the heart of Dublin. There are over four centuries of history embedded into the park, involving important Irish figures, including Countess Constance Markievicz, First Baron Ardilaun, and Arthur Guinness. Throughout the park, you will see many important monuments that are attached to Ireland's history.

Hours of operation: Monday to Saturday from 7:30 a.m. to dusk, Sundays and bank holidays from 9:30 a.m. to dusk, and Christmas Day from 9:30 a.m. to 12:30 p.m.

Merrion Square

Address: Merrion Square S, Dublin, Ireland

Merrion Square is one of Dublin's oldest and largest squares, adorned by its elegant Georgian traits dating back to the 1760s. Although the buildings are more used for office spaces, you can wander through the square and see the plaques of the building's former inhabitants. The square also has a gorgeous park in the center featuring shrub beds, an array of colorful flowers, and a statue of Oscar Wilde. If you are in Dublin on a Sunday and are looking for a leisurely morning stroll while enjoying some coffee or tea, you'll be able to peruse some artists' work as well who are selling their artwork.

Kilmainham Gaol and Courthouse

Address: Inchicore Road, Kilmainham, Dublin 8

Hours of operation: Monday to Sunday from 9:30 a.m. to 5:30 p.m.

Step back in time to the disturbing tales at Kilmainham Gaol and Courthouse, Dublin's oldest prison house dating back to 1796. This old jail housed some of Ireland's most notorious military and political leaders in Irish history until its doors closed in 1924.

The tour will give you an insight into what it was like to be a prisoner in the gaol throughout its years of operation and its involvement during the Great Famine.

The tour will last about an hour, but it is a busy attraction, so it is best to pre-book your tickets online.

Ticket type	Cost of admission
Adult	€ 8
Senior (60+)	€ 6
Child (12 to 17)	€ 4
Child under 12	Free but still needs a ticket.
Family (two adults and two or three children between 12 and 17)	€ 20

Ardgillan Castle and Gardens

Address: Ardgillan Demesne, Balbriggan, Co. Dublin

The hours of operation vary throughout the year. Use this table as your guide based on when you will be in Ireland if you are planning to visit this site.

Month	Park	Playground
January	9 a.m. to 5 p.m.	9:30 a.m. to 4:15 p.m.
February	9 a.m. to 6 p.m.	9:30 a.m. to 5:15 p.m.
March	9 a.m. to 6 p.m.	9:30 a.m. to 5:15 p.m.
April	9 a.m. to 8 p.m.	9:30 a.m. to 7:15 p.m.
May	9 a.m. to 9 p.m.	9:30 a.m. to 8:15 p.m.
June	9 a.m. to 9 p.m.	9:30 a.m. to 8:15 p.m.
July	9 a.m. to 9 p.m.	9:30 a.m. to 8:15 p.m.
August	9 a.m. to 9.m.	9:30 a.m. to 8:15 p.m.
September	9 a.m. to 8 p.m.	9:30 a.m. to 7:15 p.m.
October	9 a.m. to 8 p.m.	9:30 a.m. to 6:15 p.m.
November	9 a.m. to 5 p.m.	9:30 a.m. to 4:15 p.m.
December	9 a.m. to 5 p.m.	9:30 a.m. to 4:15 p.m.

Discover a hidden gem at the eighteenth-century Ardgillan Castle and Gardens, located about 20 miles North of Dublin City. At this free attraction, you will learn more about its history, which involves the Gaelic O'Casey Family and the Earl of Tyrconnell.

As you wander through this old country-style house, you will see some of the most spectacular views of the Irish Sea, Mourne Mountains, and Lambay Island. Outside the house's walls is a stunning Walled Garden and Rose Garden. The Walled Garden was once the kitchen garden for food supplies coming in, as well as flower arrangements.

Ardgillan Castle and Gardens is an excellent place to visit if you are traveling with children due to its fairy trail, which often excites the young. There is also afternoon tea, theater events, and a playground.

Christ Church Cathedral

Address: Christ Church Cathedral, Christchurch Place
Hours of operation (the last admission is 45 minutes before closing):

- Monday to Saturday from 9:30 a.m. to 5 p.m.
- Sunday from 12:30 p.m. to 3 p.m.

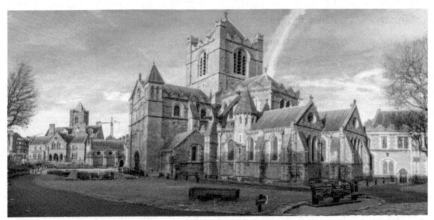

Standing in the heart of Dublin for over 1,000 years, the stunning Christ Church Cathedral is an important heritage site in the country. The church was founded in 1030 by the King of Dublin Norseman, Stiric. It was eventually incorporated into the Irish Church in 1152, where the famous Archbishop and patron saint of Dublin, Laurence O'Toole, led its practices.

You will be dazzled by the church's gorgeous architecture and floor tiles, but it's home to a famous 12-century crypt with many manuscripts and artifacts on display that will give you an idea of what worship in this cathedral in this church was once like.

This table is for the price of self-guided tours with an audio guide if you book them onsite. If you pre-book your tickets online, you will receive a discount. Guided tours are available, but you cannot book them online.

Ticket type	Price
Adult	€ 10.50
Student/Senior	€ 9
Children (4 to 12 years old)	€ 3.50
Family (two adults and two children)	€ 25
Children under 4	Free

Malahide Castle and Gardens

Address: Malahide Demesne, Malahide, Co. Dublin

Hours of operation: Monday to Sunday from 9:30 a.m. to 5:30 p.m.

Set on 250 acres of parkland, Malahide Castle is rich with history, once serving as a fortress and a home for nearly 800 years to the Talbot Family from 1185 to 1973, when the last Lord Talbot died.

The house is furnished with several pieces of furniture from different periods and a large collection of Irish portrait paintings of the Talbot family through the generations. However, the main highlights while wandering through this majestic castle are the beautiful Oak Room, which dates back to the 1600s, and the Great Hall, which dates back to 1495. There are also some memorable paintings hung in these rooms, including the Battle of the Boyne, which you will see in the Great Hall. The battle is famous in the Talbot family for the number of family members who died during the battle.

Outside, visitors can wander the beautiful Talbot Botanic Gardens, children can play on an award-winning playground, and explore a butterfly house, the ruins of an old abbey house, and a fairy trail.

Tickets can be purchased online through their website.

Ticket type	Price
Adults	€ 14.50
Children	€ 7
Family (two adults and up to three children)	€ 42
Student/Senior	€ 9.50

Drimnagh Castle

Address: Restoration Project, Long Mile Rd, Drimnagh, Walkinstown, Dublin 12

Hours of operation: Monday to Thursday from 9:30 a.m. to 4 p.m., Friday from 9:30 a.m. to 1 p.m., Closed on Saturdays and Sundays

Once the home to the de Bernival family, the Drimnagh Castle is Dublin's oldest restored castle from the Norman era and the only castle remaining that has a moat around it.

The land was given to Norman knight Hugo de Bernival and his family after they aided in the invasion of Ireland and the Crusades in 1215. Hugo de Bernival built his fortress next to what was once known as the "Crooked Glen" but is now referred to as Lansdowne Valley. The castle saw many triumphs and challenges over the centuries, including those by the O'Toole Clans, including the area evolving with businesses and the arrival of the paper mill industry.

The tour of this castle will allow you the chance to see the restored great hall with a fireplace from the 17th century, a medieval undercroft, and a battlement tower. Outside the castle, you can explore the Hornbeam Alley, lined with beautiful trees, and the Parterre garden with its symmetrical design.

If you want a tour of the castle with a guide, you will need to pre-book this in advance by contacting their office during their business hours at +01 450 2530. Tours last exactly one hour, so you must get to the castle on time. The time slots for tours are Monday to Thursday: 10 a.m., 11 a.m., 12 p.m., 1 p.m., 2 p.m. and 3 p.m., Fridays: 10 a.m., 11 a.m., 12 p.m.

Ticket type	Price*
Adult	€ 9
Student	€ 7
Child	€ 5

*Drimnagh Castle only accepts euro cash payments.

Phoenix Park

Address: Phoenix Park, Co. Dublin, Republic of Ireland

Hours of operation: The park is open 24 hours a day, all year round.

Phoenix Park is Europe's largest enclosed city park, spanning 1,750 acres. Before becoming a well-known park, Phoenix Park was a royal hunting ground in the 1660s and later opened to the public in 1747. As you explore the park, you may be lucky to see some fallow deer wandering through its expansive woods. However, you can also check out the restored Ashtown Castle from the 15th century, visit the President of Ireland's home (open on Saturdays), the Farmleigh house, the Dublin Zoo, the residence of the US Ambassador, and the Victorian People's Flower Gardens.

Iveagh Gardens

Address: St Stephen's Green, Park, Dublin 2, D02 HX65

Hours of operation: Except for March 17 and December 25, Iveagh Gardens are open daily at 8 a.m. from Monday to Saturday and at 10 a.m. on Sundays and bank holidays. The closing times vary based on daylight hours, so it's best to visit their website to confirm the closing time based on the month and week you'll be in Ireland.

Iveagh Gardens are a hidden gem in the center of Dublin, dating back to 300 years ago. These gardens aren't as well-known but were designed in 1865 with a combination of English landscape and formal French styles. Here, you will see a stunning display of fountains, rustic caves, woodlands, a rosarium, and an American garden. In addition, there are archery grounds, rockeries, and rooteries.

The Dublin Mountains

Spanning 26 miles, Dublin's Mountains make for an excellent outdoor adventure for outdoor enthusiasts. There are plenty of outdoor activities and places to explore here, with several hiking (easy to challenging) and mountain biking trails.

Shankill

Distance: Four miles (roughly 1.5 to 2 hours to complete)

Shankill is one of the shorter walks in the Dublin Mountains that will reward you with a stunning view of Dublin and the sea. As you walk along the Shankill trail, you'll wander through Rathmichael Wood and Carrickgollogan Wood, get to see the old Lead Mines Tower, enjoy the tranquil atmosphere at Barnaslingan Woods, and finish the hike where you'll see incredible views of the sea and the city.

As you hike here, you may even come across some sweet critter friends like rabbits, badgers, and birds—but remember to give them space!

Ticknock

Distance: Five miles (roughly 2 to 2.5 hours to complete)

The Ticknock trail is slightly more challenging to hike. However, following the trail, you'll wander through a beautiful forest with Japanese Larch, Sitka Spruce, Scots, Lodgepole Pine, and Monterey. As you ascend the Three Rock Mountain, you'll see the neat triple rock formation that inspired the mountain's name. As you continue your hike, you'll follow the Two Rock moorland to see some of the ruins of the Fairy Castle. You can take in stunning views of Dublin below at the highest point.

Glenasmole and Tallaght

Distance: Four miles (roughly 1.5 to 2 hours to complete)

Glenasmole and Tallaght is the final stage in the Dublin Mountains that will bring you through the gorgeous Glenasmole Valley and along the River Dodder. On this hike, you will see the Bohernabreena Waterworks, which once supplied water to the mills. When you get to Kiltipper Park, you can see the beautiful views of the Dublin Mountains.

Dublin Castle

Address: Dame St, Dublin 2

Hours of operation: Monday to Saturday from 9:45 a.m. to 4:45 p.m., Sunday from 12 p.m. to 4:45 p.m., The last admission is at 4:15 p.m., Dublin Castle is closed from December 25 to 27, and January 1

Dublin Castle has served for just about every purpose you can think of. Built-in the 13th century on a Viking settlement by King John of England, the castle has had various purposes over its years, including serving as a military fortress, prison, treasury, court of law, and the former seat of the English Administration until Ireland split into two countries. You'll get to wander through its ancient walls, learning about its intricate history and how it was the focal point during the night during the Easter Rising in 1916. The gardens outside of the castle walls are also something to marvel at.

Guided tours are available and run for one hour.

Ticket type	Guided tour	Unguided tour
Adult	€ 10	€ 7
Student/Senior	€ 8	€ 6
Child (6 to 17 years old)	€ 4	€ 3
Child (under 6)	Free	Free

Things to Enjoy in Dublin

Dublin has plenty of places to explore, but it's also important to find some things to enjoy on your travels!

Royal Hibernian Academy

Address: Gallagher Gallery, 15 Ely Place, Co Dublin
Hours of operation: Monday to Saturday from 11 a.m. to 5 p.m. except on Wednesdays when the gallery closes at 6:30 p.m., Sundays from 12 p.m. to 5 p.m.

If you enjoy visual arts, a trip to the Royal Hibernian Academy is a must! This institution loves helping artists shape their craft following traditional and innovative approaches to making their work unique.

There is a lot to explore on the five floors of the gallery, including curated works from Irish and international art and emerging artists who have yet to establish themselves in Dublin. There is no entry fee for the gallery.

National Museum of Ireland—Natural History

Address: Natural History, Merrion Street, Dublin 2, D02 F627

Hours of operation: Tuesday to Saturday from 10 a.m. to 5 p.m., Sunday and Monday from 1 a.m. to 5 p.m.

The National Museum of Ireland—Natural History has plenty of things to do for the whole family. This museum has been around since 1857 and has galleries filled with animals from Ireland and around the world, geological exhibits containing over two million scientific specimens (about half are insects), and much more! It's a perfect way to spend a rainy day in Ireland and take in some fascinating scientific wonders from over the years.

There is no entry fee to enter the museum.

Guinness Storehouse

It wouldn't be a trip to Dublin without visiting the Guinness Storehouse to learn more and taste a pint of Ireland's famous beer!

Enjoy a self-guided tour of the storehouse, exploring the seven floors of the building that once served as the fermentation plant. You will also learn more about the history of Guinness, its culture, the ingredients that go into this iconic stout, and how to pour the perfect pint of Guinness. Finish it off with a selfie printed onto the head of your pint!

If you want a private tour, you can check out the Connoisseur Experience, which will still give you Guinness's history. However, you'll also get to sample four of their popular beers brewed by Guinness while touring the building.

Standard Tours

Tickets can be purchased online through the Guinness Storehouse website. Tickets are not available for the Guinness Storehouse plus STOUTie or Guinness Academy upgrades.

Ticket type	Guinness Storehouse	Guinness Storehouse plus STOUTie	Guinness Storehouse plus Guinness Academy
Adult	€ 20	€ 28	€ 32
Student (18+)/senior (65+)	€ 17	€ 23	€ 26
Child (5 to 17 years old)	€ 10	NA	NA
Child (under four)	Free	NA	NA
Family (two adults and two children)	€ 51	€ 64	€ 70

Premium Tours

Premium Tours are only available for visitors who are 18 and older. These tours last up to three hours.

Experience Package	Price
Connoisseur experience	€ 95
The Guinness Brewery experience	€ 280

Chester Beatty

Address: Chester Beatty, Dublin Castle, Dublin 2, D02 AD92

Hours of operation: Tuesday to Friday from 9:45 a.m. to 5:30 p.m., Wednesday from 9:45 a.m. to 8 p.m., Saturday from 9:45 a.m. to 5:30 p.m., Sunday from 12 p.m. to 5:30 p.m., Closed: January 1, Good Friday, and from December 24 to 26

Journey through the different continents as you wander the Chester Beatty Museum, exhibiting a collection of artistic treasures from the Middle East, North Africa, Asia, and Europe. You will get to see a diverse collection of art, manuscripts, prints, drawings, and so much more from these corners of the world, all donated by Sir Alfred Chester Beatty, an American mining magnate and philanthropist. This museum is a fantastic way to spend a few hours to learn more about different cultures!

Admission to Chester Beatty is free, and tours are self-guided. Guided tours are available on specific times and dates and are free but must be pre-booked.

EPIC The Irish Emigration Museum

Address: CHQ, Custom House Quay, Dublin 1

Hours of operation: 10 a.m. to 6:45 p.m. daily (the last entry is at 5 p.m.)

Take the time to learn and understand the Irish culture and history at EPIC, the Irish Emigration Museum. At this interactive museum, you will experience what it means to be Irish, expanding to many stories of Irish emigrants who became politicians, poets, artists, and scientists.

Additionally, you can learn about why many left the island, where they moved to, and what they brought with them in that move. This museum can also help you learn more about your Irish ancestry, where you can see records and speak with a genealogy expert who will help you further understand your roots and family connections. This is a fantastic experience to check out if you have the time! All ticket prices reflected are if you book online.

Self-Guided Experiences

Self-guided experiences allow you to experience the museum on your own.

General Admission

Ticket type	Price
Adult (18 to 64 years old)	€ 19.50
Teen (13 to 17 years old)	€ 13
Child (6 to 12 years old)	€ 10
Student (16 and up with proof)	€ 17
Senior (65 and up)	€ 17.50
Audio guide	€ 2

Families

Ticket type	Price
Two adults and two children	€ 49
Two adults and one child	€ 42
One adult and two children	€ 34
One adult and one child	€ 28
Additional child	€ 8
Audio guide	€ 2

Guided Experiences
Daily guided tours are an hour long, running at 1 p.m. daily. Adults: €22 and Children: €11.50

Private Tours
Private tours give you an in-depth experience in the museum for a maximum of six people. For two people: €210; additional people: €22

Combo Experiences
EPIC Museum and Jeanie Johnston Famine Ship

This combo experience gives you a guided tour of the Jeanie Johnston ship in addition to an entrance to the museum afterward.

Ticket type	Price
Adult	€ 30
Teen	€ 21.50
Child	€ 16
Student/Senior	€ 26.60
Infant	Free

EPIC and Urban Brewing Beer Paddle

Experience a paddle of beer before or after you wander through EPIC. Please note that the brewery is closed on Mondays. The price is €31.50 per adult.

Genealogy Experiences
If you're wanting to discover your Irish roots, this is an amazing experience. There are three options to choose from, two of which can be done in person.

Consultation type	Online	In-person
30-minute consultation	€ 70	NA
50-minute consultation	€ 121	€ 121
80-minute consultation	€ 172	€ 172

The Zoological Museum

Address: College Green, Dublin 2, Ireland

The Zoological Museum is an interactive museum experience with a history of over 250 years. During this experience, you can hold a narwhal tusk, see the skull of a hippo, and take a photo with a great white shark's jaw. If you or a family member are brave, you can hold a live frog, snake, insect, and a few other things on display!

For more information on hours of operation and admission prices, please check their website at https://www.tcd.ie/Zoology.

Jameson Distillery Bow St.

Address: Bow St, Smithfield, Dublin 7, D07 N9VH

Hours of operation: Monday to Thursday from 10 a.m. to 6 p.m., Friday and Saturday from 10 a.m. to 7 p.m., Sundays from 12 p.m. to 6 p.m.

The former Jameson Distillery factory is a monument to Irish history, dating back to 1780 when John Jameson founded the company.

A visit to the distillery will give you a tour of the former factory and other optional experiences, including premium whiskey tasting, making cocktails, and how to blend your whiskey!

As the legal drinking age in Ireland is 18, visitors 17 and under can only participate in the Bow Street Experience.

Bow Street Experience—45 Minutes
€26 per person

Take a 45-minute tour of the Jameson Distillery, learning more about the history of John Jameson and the iconic whiskey well-known in Ireland and around the world, complete with a whiskey tasting along the way!

If you want to up this experience, there is the Bow Street experience and a cask draw where you can taste whiskey right from its barrel! That experience is €41 per person. Children will not be allowed in this experience if you decide to go for the cask draw.

Jameson Black Barrel Blending Class—90 Minutes
€60 per person

The Jameson black barrel blending class will teach you how to blend your own whiskey to take home. This tour does not include a guided tour.

Whiskey Cocktail Making Class—60 Minutes
€55 per person

Spend an hour learning and tasting three cocktails mixed with Jameson whiskey. You will get all the tools you need to make a yummy whiskey sour, old-fashioned, and Jameson punch!

Secret Whiskey Tasting—One Hour
€40 per person

Step inside John Jameson's office and join a Jameson Ambassador as you learn about the history of Jameson Whiskey and some other hidden secrets as you sample whiskey.

The Taste Table—90 Minutes
€140 per person

Take a unique journey as you spend time in Jameson's maturation warehouse (the only one in Ireland). You will get to sample popular whiskey brands, including Midleton Very Rare Barry Crockett, Redbreast, and Red Spot, plus an exclusive and rate whiskey from a barrel. You'll also get to enjoy chocolates that pair perfectly with each whiskey!

Jameson Black Barrel Bottle Your Own—Five Minutes
€120 per person

Take your own Jameson home that you bottled! You will get a personalized label to add to your bottle. This experience is only available from Monday to Saturday at 10:30 a.m. and on Sundays at 12:30 p.m. This experience cannot be pre-booked in advance.

The Book of Kells and Old Library

Address: The University of Dublin Trinity College, College Green, Dublin

Hours of operation: Monday to Saturday from 9:30 a.m. to 5 p.m., Sundays from 12 p.m. to 4:30 p.m.

Trinity College is the oldest university in Ireland and houses the most famous religious manuscript from the ninth century, the Book of Kells. This ancient manuscript contains the first four gospels of the New Testament, handwritten in Latin. You can see this in Trinity College's Old Library before further checking out other important historical pieces, such as an original copy of the Proclamation and Ireland's oldest harp, the Brian Boru Harp.

Must try food in Dublin

Irish Stew: This hearty dish is a classic in Irish cuisine. It typically consists of

lamb or mutton, potatoes, onions, and carrots, all slow-cooked in a savory broth flavored with herbs like thyme and parsley. Irish stew is a perfect comfort food, especially on a chilly day.

Boxty: Boxty is a traditional Irish potato pancake that can be served as a side dish

or a main course. It's made with grated potatoes, mashed potatoes, flour, and buttermilk. The mixture is fried until crispy on the outside and soft on the inside. Boxty can be enjoyed with various toppings, such as bacon, eggs, or smoked salmon.

Coddle: Coddle is a Dublin specialty and a comforting one-pot meal. It typically

includes pork sausages, bacon, onions, and potatoes, all stewed together in a seasoned broth. Coddle has been a favorite among Dubliners for generations and is often served with a slice of crusty bread.

Seafood Chowder: Ireland's coastal location means that it has an abundance of

fresh seafood, and Dublin is no exception. Seafood chowder, a creamy soup filled with various types of fish, shrimp, mussels, and sometimes smoked salmon, is a delightful treat for seafood lovers. Enjoy it with a side of brown bread for a complete meal.

Where to Stay in Dublin

Whether you're staying in Dublin for one night, two nights, or three, you will want to stay in a place that is relatively central in the city to make it easier to get to the different attractions and experiences you want to go to:

The Green: Located in Stephen's Green, The Green is a mid-range hotel close to Iveagh Gardens, Dublin Castle, and Trinity College. This hotel offers a buffet breakfast to start your day in addition to a restaurant with a range of international dishes.

Marlin Hotel Stephen's Green: Marlin Hotel Stephen's Green is near Dublin Castle and St. Stephen's Green. It's also a mid-range hotel but offers a full English or Irish breakfast each morning.

Clontarf Castle Hotel: Feel like royalty when you stay at the stunning Clontarf Castle Hotel! This luxury hotel is 10 minutes outside Dublin and offers a tranquil setting away from the busy city.

Garden Lane Backpackers: If you're traveling to Ireland on a budget, the Garden Lane Backpackers is an excellent hostel. All rooms have a wardrobe for your belongings. It's also near major attractions like the Guinness Storehouse.

The Croke Park Hotel: Situated just outside of Dublin near Croke Park Stadium, the Croke Park Hotel is a mid-range accommodation offering comfortable rooms and a beautiful restaurant serving European cuisine with all fresh ingredients.

Generator Dublin: The Generator Dublin is a Smithfield Square hostel next door to Jameson Distillery and steps to many other major attractions in Dublin. This hostel allows you to stay in dorm rooms, quads, or a private ensuite to fit your traveling needs.

Sea View D4: If you're looking for bed and breakfast accommodation in Dublin, located in the suburb of Ballsbridge. This bed and breakfast has stunning sea views and is less than one mile from The Book of Kells at The Old Library. You will receive a continental breakfast each morning, or you can have room service.

Tipperary House Dublin: The Tipperary House Dublin is a low-cost option near many of Dublin's main attractions. There are various room options, including twin rooms or dorms, which work out well depending on the type of traveler you are!

What NOT to do in Dublin

There are so many things to do in Dublin that it's easy to remember some of the things you shouldn't do while traveling around the city and its surrounding areas. Here are some things you should avoid as a tourist while in Dublin.

Don't Get a Drink at the Temple Bar
The Temple Bar is a popular spot for tourists, especially since it's one of the oldest pubs in Dublin. However, although it is a hot spot for tourists to go to, you're not going to experience the most authentic Irish vibe as you might in other low-key pubs—plus, you're going to pay a pretty penny for that pint of Guinness and be smooshed in with the crowd. You're better off looking for a pint elsewhere in Dublin where it's not as busy, such as The Brazen Head or The Cobblestone.

Don't Expect to Party All Night Long
Pubs don't stay open late in Dublin (or Ireland). Most close at 11:30 p.m. on a weeknight and 1 a.m. on the weekend.

Don't Go to St. Patrick's Day Events in the Evening
Unless you're prepared to be around very drunk people, don't attend St. Patrick's Day celebrations in the evening. Instead, join in on the festivities during the day and then have an early night in.

Don't Pay for Too Many Attractions
While you have been given a list of great places to check out, remember that Dublin is a pricey city to visit! Decide which places would be high on your list to go, and keep your budget for other spots you're going to around the country. Instead, use the free museums and galleries to immerse yourself in neat experiences!

Remember that many of these attractions are closed on Mondays, but it's best to verify on their websites.

Don't Stick to Dublin's City Center
Dublin has many things to do and see, but don't stick to the city center! There are so many great outdoor things to do outside the city limits, such as exploring the Dublin Mountains!

Don't Drink Guinness or Whiskey if You're Not a Fan of It
Guinness and whiskey are not for everyone, and that's okay! If you're not a fan, you don't have to drink a pint of Guinness or have whiskey. There are plenty of other alcoholic and nonalcoholic beverages you can enjoy, including other beers from different local breweries.

Don't Go to Grafton Street
Most tourist books and leaflets will tell you to visit Grafton Street because it is a large pedestrian shopping area. However, the shops are chain stores you'll likely find anywhere else. If you're looking for an area with independent shops, walk a few streets to the Creative Quarter, where you will find some of the cutest shops with unique finds!

Don't Buy Souvenirs
Souvenirs are tempting to buy but are commercial and not reflective of the city you're visiting (including Dublin). Instead of buying souvenirs at tourist chains, shop at independent shops where you can find interesting souvenirs to bring home!

A trip to Ireland's capital will be exciting, with a rich history and culture, a welcoming atmosphere, and a stunning backdrop. There are many things to experience and enjoy in Dublin, including touring the historical landmarks and wandering through the beautiful castles and gardens. No matter your interests, Dublin will captivate you with its charm and character!

Chapter 4:

Belfast—Dos and Don'ts

Although it's Northern Ireland's biggest city and capital, Belfast has a rich history and vibrant culture paired with stunning architecture and warm hospitality that will leave a lasting impression. Of course, the first thing that comes to anyone's mind is Belfast's connection to the RMS Titanic; this is the city to go to if you are looking to explore and experience a lively arts scene, a buzzing nightlife, and see the various places where Game of Thrones was filmed. Let's look at some locations you should consider exploring and experiencing while in Belfast.

What to DO in Belfast

With Belfast so rich in history and plenty of things to do, where do you start? This section will look at the top highlights of what to do in Belfast.

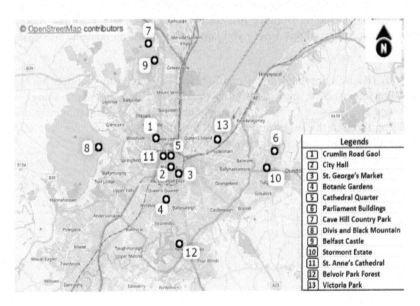

Legends
1 Crumlin Road Gaol
2 City Hall
3 St. George's Market
4 Botanic Gardens
5 Cathedral Quarter
6 Parliament Buildings
7 Cave Hill Country Park
8 Divis and Black Mountain
9 Belfast Castle
10 Stormont Estate
11 St. Anne's Cathedral
12 Belvoir Park Forest
13 Victoria Park

Crumlin Road Gaol

Address: 53-55 Crumlin Road, Belfast, BT14 6ST

Hours of operation: 10 a.m. to 6 p.m. daily. The last admission times are as follows: Sunday to Thursday at 4 p.m., Friday and Saturday from September to March at 4 p.m., and then 4:30 p.m. from April to August.

The Crumlin Road Gaol is a jail dating back to the nineteenth century that now serves as a location for tours, concerts, and other events. This jail opened its cell doors to prisoners in 1846 and closed its doors on March 31, 1996. In the years of its running as a prison, Crumlin Road Gaol kept murderers, suffragettes, loyalists, and republic prisoners behind bars.

Self-Guided Tour

Take yourself on a walk through the Crumlin Road Gaol. You will get to walk through many different areas of the Gaol, including the tunnel, the historic holding cells, and the hangman's cell. This tour is unique as it will also include video, audio, and holograms throughout your tour, giving you an insight into life as a prisoner and staff member at the jail.

Ticket type	Door Price	Online price
Adult	£14.50	£14
Student/Senior	£13	£12.50
Child	£8	£7.50
Family of four (maximum of two adults)	£40	£38

Guided Gaol Experience

The guided gaol experience is a 90-minute guided tour that will take you through all of Crumlin Road's history, where you will learn all about the prisoners and executions that were carried out. You'll also learn why the prison was closed in 1996. In addition to seeing the areas you will see if you take a self-guided tour, you will also get to go through exclusive areas that aren't on the self-guided tour. The price for the guided tour is £19.50 per person.

Belfast City Hall

Address: Donegall Square, Belfast, County Antrim, BT1 5GS

Hours of operation: Monday to Friday from 8:30 a.m. to 5 p.m., Saturday and Sunday from 10 a.m. to 5 p.m.

Until the 1600s, Belfast was a small settlement. However, given its place on the island, it quickly grew into a more industrialized area, earning its upgraded status to a small town in 1613. Belfast began to grow with more and more people moving to the town, and by 1801, it was home to a population of 20,000 people. The population began to grow over the years, and by 1888, Queen Victoria decided to update Belfast's status to a city, and it was agreed that a building would need to be established to reflect the new status. Belfast's City Hall was constructed in 1898, opening its doors on August 1, 1906.

The interior of the building is stunning. You will see different types of marble used, showing no expense was spared. Several paintings and beautiful stained-glass windows commemorate the important pieces of Belfast's history. Two of the most important stained-glass pieces feature King Edward VII and Queen Alexandria, who reigned when City Hall officially opened its doors. On his deathbed, there is also a dramatic marble sculpture of Frederick Richard Chichester, the last Earl of Donegall.

Outside the building, you can wander through the Titanic Memorial Garden, which features several monuments and memorials to the iconic ship of dreams.

You can tour Belfast City Hall on your own or with a guide. If you choose to take a guided tour, it is on a first-come, first-serve basis.

St. George's Market

Address: 12-20 East Bridge Street, Belfast, County Antrim, BT1 3NQ
Hours of operation: Fridays from 8 a.m. to 2 p.m., Saturdays from 9 a.m. to 3 p.m., Sundays from 10 a.m. to 3 p.m.

St. George's Market is Belfast's oldest and is highly rated in the UK and Ireland. This market has been around since the 1600s. However, the existing award-winning market was constructed between 1890 and 1896. This market is excellent to visit if you want to purchase fresh produce, find unique gifts and souvenirs, and listen to some local musicians. Each day has a theme:

St. George's Market Fridays have various vendors, including fresh fish stalls, produce, and antiques.

Saturdays at the St. George's Market are called The Saturday City Food and Craft Market. Here, you can buy all sorts of good eats from all over the world, check out craft vendors, and much more.

Sundays at the St George's Market have a mix of local arts and crafts, antiques, and much more!

Botanic Garden

Address: College Park, Botanic Avenue, Belfast, County Antrim, BT7 1LP
Hours of operation: 7:30 a.m. to 5 p.m. daily

Established in 1828, Belfast's Botanic Gardens is a prime example of important Victorian history, built in response to the public's interest in botany and horticulture. Housed inside a beautiful glasshouse, you will see a collection of exotic trees and stunning flowers from the southern hemisphere in the Tropical Ravine and Palm House. The work that has gone into cultivating and keeping the various unusual plant species in the greenhouse environment is worth learning about, especially when you can see some of the oldest seed plants in the world, flowering vines, and much more!

There is no cost to visit the Botanic Garden.

Cathedral Quarter

The Cathedral Quarter in Belfast is home to some of Belfast's oldest buildings, interesting art galleries, and some of the best pubs and restaurants (making it perfect for a night out). However, before it became the area it is today, it was once the warehousing and trading point in the city. As you wander through this area, you'll see plenty of these buildings still standing today. One of the places worth checking out is the Merchant Hotel. This hotel is stunning with its nineteenth-century architecture. It's still a working hotel today, but you don't need to stay here to appreciate its beauty, especially the chandelier in the Great Room!

St. Anne's Cathedral

Address: Donegall Street, Belfast, County Antrim, BT1 2HB
Hours of operation: Monday to Friday from 10:30 a.m. to 4 p.m.

St. Anne's Cathedral, also known as Belfast Cathedral, can be found in the Cathedral Quarter and has been a central place for Christian worship for over 100 years. This church is home to the famous Spire of Hope, stunning stonework sculpted by Rosamond Praeger, Esmond Burton, and Morris Harding, elaborate mosaics by the Martin sisters, and beautiful stained glass windows. There is a small admission fee to visit (£2 per person), and the church tours are self-guided unless you plan a guided tour. This church is also still a working church and has regular services.

Parliament Buildings

Address: Upper Newtownards Road, Belfast, County Antrim, BT4 3XX

Hours of operation: Monday to Friday from 9 a.m. to 4 p.m. (except on public and bank holidays). Parliament Buildings in Belfast are the home of the Northern Ireland Assembly, which serves as the legislative body for Northern Ireland.

When Sir Arnold Thornley of Liverpool was designing the building, it was to involve three different buildings on the grounds, which spanned about 224 acres at the time of the Stormont Estate being purchased. However, due to the rising cost of materials, among other expenses, the plans changed to constructing only one building, but the name with the pluralized word, buildings, stayed. The construction began in 1921, and the Parliament Buildings were officially opened on November 16, 1932, by then Prince of Wales Edward VIII.

The building is grand on the outside with its classical Greek design. You can also see where the other buildings would have been constructed had the costs not been as high during its construction.

The tour of the building is self-guided. However, if you want to join a public tour, they are available from Monday to Friday at 11 a.m. and 2 p.m., and tickets need to be booked, which can be done online through the Northern Ireland Assembly website.

As this is still a working building, you can expect it to be busy and noisy, especially on Mondays and Tuesdays when the Assembly sits in council.

Stormont Estate

Address: Upper Newtownards Road, Belfast, County Antrim, BT43TA

Hours of operation: Monday to Friday from 7:30 a.m. to 6 p.m., Saturday and Sunday from 9 a.m. to 5 p.m. The Mo Mowlam Play Park is open daily from 9:30 a.m. to 4:30 p.m.

The stunning Stormont Estate is a park surrounded by beautiful gardens, walking trails, and a children's playground (The Mo Mowlam Play Park). Around the park and estate are plenty of historic buildings, memorials, statues, and World War II sites, including the barrage balloon anchors that held balloons in place to protect buildings during the bombings.

If your kids want to play for a while, the Mo Mowlam Play Park is an inclusive playground that allows children of all abilities to play together. For kids that need more quiet time, visit the park on a Sunday between 9:30 a.m. and 10:30 a.m. for the park's quiet hour.

Cave Hill County Park

Hours of operation: The park opens daily at 7:30 a.m. However, closing times will vary based on when sunset is.

Park entrances:

- Upper Cavehill Road entrance, BT15 5FB
- Upper Hightown Road entrance and car park, BT14 8RR
- Innisfayle Park entrance and car park, Antrim Road BT15 5GR
- Horseshoe Bend entrance, Crumlin Road, BT14 8QU
- Grays Lane entrance and car park, Antrim Road BT15 4EP
- Carrs Glen entrance, Ballysillan Road BT14 8LA
- Hazelwood entrance, beside Belfast Zoo BT36 7PN

Cave Hill Country Park is Belfast's biggest park, visible from nearly everywhere in the city. This is an excellent attraction if you're looking for outdoor activities. In this park, you can check out several geological, archaeological, and historical sites, including the remains of a stone circle and McArt's Fort.

Cave Hill Country Park has three trails you can walk along and vary in difficulty levels. They are

Cavehill Trail is a 4.5-mile circular walking route. This trail will take you to McArt's Fort. If you plan to walk this trail, you will want to ensure you wear sturdy walking shoes and be prepared for the ascent, as it is 256 meters.

Estate Trail is a 2.4-mile circular walking route. This trail will take you through the woodland and follow paths on the lower slopes of the park. The ascent of this trail is 134 meters.

Castle Trail which is the shortest circular trail at just under one mile. This trail will take you to the gardens at Belfast Castle.

No matter which trails you wander through, you will be rewarded with some stunning panoramic views of Belfast. In addition, this park will also bring you to the Belfast Zoo, which kids love, as well as an adventure playground.

Belfast Castle

Address: Antrim Road, Belfast, County Antrim, BT15 5GR

Hours of operation: 9 a.m. to 6 p.m. daily

Northern Ireland's iconic landmark, Belfast Castle, is along the Cave Hill Country Park. The first castle was built in the Norman era in the city center during the twelfth century, followed by a second one constructed by Sir Arthur Chichester, the Baron of Belfast, at the same site in 1611. Unfortunately, the second castle burnt down nearly 100 years later, with only the street names (Castle Place, Castle Street, Castle Lane, and Castle Arcade) to mark its former location.

A new castle was planned in 1862 and built by 1870 by the third Marquis of Donegall, a descendant of the Chichester family. After his death, the castle and estate were passed to his son-in-law, Lord Ashley, the seventh Earl of Shaftesbury. Belfast remained in the Shaftesbury family until they passed the estate and the building over to the city in 1934.

The building is impressive to visitors, giving them a stunning view of the park and area. Walking in through the door, you'll see that much of the ground and first floor have retained their original features. Outside are some well-maintained woodlands and gardens to wander through and take pictures.

There is no admission fee to Belfast Castle.

Divis and the Black Mountains

Address: Divis Road, Hannahstown, near Belfast, County Antrim, BT17 0NG

Hours of operation vary based on the time of the year. It's best to check online based on the day you intend to go.

Enjoy some stunning panoramic views of Belfast, County Ulster in the Republic of Ireland, and parts of England and Scotland from the Divis and Black Mountains. These mountains are located in Belfast Hills and are the background setting to Belfast's skyline. There are plenty of walking trails for different fitness levels to follow and archaeological remains to discover along the way. In addition, this area is home to many flora, fauna, and other wildlife. Here are the different trails you can follow:

Lough Trail: The Lough Trail is easy to follow if you're looking for an effortless walk. This trail is 0.9 miles long and will give you views of the Lough Neagh toward the Sperrin Mountains and Collin Valley near the Mourne Mountains. You will start this walk by the Long Barn. Next to it, you will see the remains of a homestead used in World War II as a rifle range.

Summit Trail: The Summit Trail is a challenging three-mile hike that will bring you to the summit of Divis Mountain. At the peak (and if it's a clear day), you'll see Scotland, Donegal, Cumbria, Isle of Man, and Wales. To get to the Summit Trail, you will need to follow the way-marked Tipperary Road trail, then turn left at the Long Barn.

Ridge Trail: The Ridge Trail is a moderate gravel and stone-pitched trail spanning 4.2 miles. This trail will take you toward the Divis transmitter masts and along a wooden boardwalk toward the Black Mountain summit. On a clear day, you will be able to see Scotland, Cumbria, and the Isle of Man. You will hang a right at the Divis Lodge next to the Long Barn to get to the hike.

Trail maps can be found on the Belfast Hills Partnership website. However, you can find this information in the book's reference section.

Belvoir Park Forest

Address: Belvoir Drive, Belfast, County Antrim, BT8 7QT
Hours of operation: Belvoir Park Forest is open 24 hours a day all year round.

A trip to the Belvoir Park Forest is a must if you're looking for a lovely outdoor adventure in a forest. This park was opened to the public in 1961 and is within a forest spanning along the River Lagan for about 185 acres.

As you walk through the forest, you will see many nods to its history. If you drive to the park, you'll see a raised piece of ground called a motte where castles were built from the twelfth century, dating back to John de Courcy during his invasion of Ulster. There is also an Ice House built into the motte's side. In addition, Shaw's Bridge helped Cromwell's gunners cross the river and the ruins of the Irish Ring Fort.

At one point, the forest was home to a small community where you could see the tiny village's ruins. There is also a medieval graveyard with gravesites from the fourteenth century (which is somewhat remarkable given how long ago that was).

In addition to seeing some of the historical elements, there is a 1.5-mile loop you can walk around. However, if you fancy a longer stroll, head to the Lagan Valley Regional Park, which is connected to Belvoir Park Forest.

Victoria Park

Address: Park Avenue, Belfast, County Antrim, BT4 1JT
Hours of operation: Victoria Park is open 24 hours a day all year round.

Victoria Park in Belfast was opened to the public on September 15, 1906, to replace another park on the former Dargan Island (which is now Queen's Island). This park has a lovely lake that was once used for boating and two small wooden islands for swans and ducks.

In addition to some of its wildlife, Victoria Park has playing fields for football, a lawn bowling green, and a track for cycling and BMX.

Things to Enjoy in Belfast

As you explore Belfast and its historical sites and stunning parks, remember to immerse yourself in some other essential pieces of its history. Remember, Titanic is linked to Belfast, and this is the city where you can learn more about her roots and do other fun things!

Titanic Belfast

Address: Titanic Belfast, 1 Olympic Way, Queen's Road, Belfast, County Antrim, BT3 9EP

Hours of operation: The opening times for the museum vary based on the time of the year. Please check their website to confirm based on when you plan to be in Belfast.

Admission: Adults: £24.95, Children: £11

When Titanic set sail on her maiden voyage to New York City, she was called the ship of dreams. Her tragic ending on the fateful night of April 14, 1912, is one story that fascinates many of us, mainly because she was meant to be unsinkable.

Step into her iconic history in the world's largest Titanic museum at Titanic Belfast. The museum will take you through the story of RMS Titanic and her sister ships, the Olympic and Britannic, and their design and construction until Titanic set sail. The museum will also give you insight into the trial and inquest that followed her sinking to the bottom of the Atlantic Ocean.

There are nine interpretive and interactive galleries to explore at the museum, including the ability to experience the sights, sounds, smells, and stories of the Titanic. It's a really neat experience for all ages!

SS Nomadic

When the RMS Titanic set out on her maiden voyage, she had yet to pick up some of her passengers—this is where the help of the SS Nomadic came in. The Nomadic was the tender for the Titanic and ferried over the first and second-class passengers to board the Titanic from Cherbourg as the dockside was too shallow for the Titanic to dock. With her rich history and important job, she is worth exploring, especially since her recent restoration to how she looked in 1911. She is the only remaining ship from the White Star Line in the world!

Even after the Titanic sank, the Nomadic still had important tasks during both World Wars, carrying thousands of passengers to other major transatlantic liners and serving as a restaurant and party venue in Paris next to the Eiffel Tower.

When you climb aboard the Nomadic, you'll experience and feel what it was like to be in your respective classes along the four decks from her time as a ferry to her days as a restaurant. She has seen so much in her many years of service!

Tickets to see the SS Nomadic are included with your Titanic Experience tickets.

Ulster Museum

Address: Botanic Gardens, Belfast, County Antrim, BT9 5AB

Hours of operation: 10 a.m to 5 p.m. daily

Step into the Ulster Museum to learn a collection of stories that connect the dots to who Northern Ireland is, including the perspectives of ancient Ireland, global histories, the Troubles, and what the country's future may hold.

The museum has interactive discovery centers that offer a unique learning experience in art, history, and nature, which is fun for any age. You will get to hold some of the most exciting items in their collections in their discovery centers. However, if you are going to Ireland during the school year, it may not be possible to access the discovery centers if schools book them.

No pre-booking is required for the museum, and it is a free attraction.

Grand Opera House

Address: Great Victoria Street, Belfast, County Antrim, BT2 7HR

Box office hours of operation: 10 a.m. to 5 p.m. daily

The Grand Opera House in Belfast was designed and built by the famous architect Frank Matcham in 1895 and is the only Victorian theater in Northern Ireland.

Since its opening, the theater has seen many changes, from its name to becoming a repertory theater during the Second World War. It was the place where a gala performance was held after the war ended. If you want to learn more, you can check out their Heritage Exhibition, which showcases the history of the Grand Opera House from its construction to its use today. You'll learn more about Matcham, see photos of the various performers, and a collection of other memorabilia.

If you want to learn more from one of the theater's experts, there are guided tours you can join before wandering through the Heritage Exhibition. The expert will be able to take you behind the scenes of the theater and give you an in-depth history lesson of the restored theater as well as some of the famous performers to take the stage.

Tours run from 45 minutes to an hour.

Tour dates and times: Saturdays at 10:30 a.m. and 12 p.m.

Tour ticket prices: Adults: £12.50, Children: £9

Belfast Bus Tour

Hours of operation: 10 a.m. to 3 p.m. daily. Tours operate every 45 minutes from Monday to Friday and every 20 to 30 minutes on Saturday and Sunday. If you don't hop on and off, the tour will last between 75 and 90 minutes.

Taking a tour of Belfast on a bus is one of the best ways to enjoy panoramic views of the city with commentary from a tour guide. The bus will take you around the city, stopping at 19 major attractions, including the Titanic Belfast, St. George's Market, and Crumlin Road Gaol. This is a great way to get around the city and from the various attractions you want to visit.

In addition, there are other daily coastal tours you can look into, including a Game of Thrones Sightseeing Tour, which will take you to the locations where Game of Thrones was filmed.

Tickets can be pre-booked online through the City Tours Belfast website. You will also find all the information needed for the various bus stops.

Belfast Zoo

Address: Antrim Road, Belfast, County Antrim, BT36 7PN

Hours of operation:

From October 1 to March 30: 10 a.m. to 4 p.m. (animal houses close at 3 p.m. and last entry is at 2:30 p.m.)

From March 31 to September 30: 10 a.m. to 6 p.m. (animal houses close at 6 p.m. and last entry is at 4:30 p.m.)

Belfast Zoo is home to more than 120 species and 800 animals from around the world, many of which are endangered. Here, you can see some beloved animals, including the African pygmy goat, American guinea pig, Malayan sun bear, Mossy frog, ostrich, white-breasted barn animal, and so much more! If you're curious to learn more about these animals, check out their feeding times, as the zookeepers will give you more insight into how they care for the animals!

Tickets can be bought at the zoo. However, if you book them online, you'll get a small discount. The prices listed in the table are reflective of buying tickets online.

Ticket type	Price
Adults	£13.50
Child (4 to 16 years old)	£6.75
Student/Senior (both require valid ID)	£6.75
Children under 4	free
Family (two adults and up to three children)	£38.50
Carers*	Free

*Carers are not required to book a ticket in advance. However, to gain free access to the zoo, proper documentation must be provided, such as a doctor's note or other relevant paperwork. Alternatively, the visitor who needs a carer can show evidence of their disability.

Must try food in Belfast

Ulster Fry: Ulster Fry is Northern Ireland's version of a traditional Irish breakfast. It typically includes fried eggs, bacon, sausages, black and white

pudding, baked beans, grilled tomatoes, and sometimes fried potato bread or soda bread. It's a hearty and filling breakfast that will keep you energized throughout the day.

Champs: Champ is a simple yet flavorful dish made from mashed potatoes,

scallions (green onions), butter, and milk. It's a classic Irish side dish that pairs well with a variety of main courses. The creamy texture and the subtle onion flavor make champ a comforting and satisfying accompaniment to many meals.

Yellowman: For dessert, try Yellowman, a traditional honeycomb toffee that is  crunchy and sweet. It's a treat that has been enjoyed in Northern Ireland for centuries, especially during fairs and festivals. The golden, crunchy candy is a delightful way to satisfy your sweet tooth and experience a taste of Belfast's culinary history.

Belfast Bap: A Belfast bap is a large, soft bread roll that's commonly used in sandwiches. You can find a variety of fillings inside these baps, ranging from traditional ham and cheese to more contemporary options like pulled pork or seafood. The bap is a staple of Belfast street food and is perfect for a quick and tasty meal on the go.

Where to Stay in Belfast

No matter how long you plan to be in Belfast, plenty of accommodations are available for any budget. It all depends on what you want to do and see while you're here. These hotels listed are mid-range for the most part. Of course, if you're looking for self-catering accommodations, Airbnb is another option to check out based on how long you plan to stay in Belfast.

Staying in Titanic Quarter

The Titanic Quarter is near the shipyard where the famous RMS Titanic was built. There are plenty of things to explore and do in this area, including the Titanic Belfast and SS Nomadic! There are only two hotels in this area:

Titanic Hotel: The Titanic Hotel is more on the luxury side of accommodations overlooking the waterfront. However, it's perfect for any traveler, even families and those who need accessible accommodations. This hotel will provide additional bedding for children if needed and a delicious breakfast! You can find this hotel on Queens Road in the Titanic Quarter.

Premier Inn Belfast Titanic Quarter Hotel: The Premier Inn Belfast Titanic Quarter Hotel is perfect for travelers sticking to a budget. This hotel offers double rooms and premium rooms that are comfortable. It's also near many of the attractions in the Titanic Quarter, including the Titanic Belfast. You can find this hotel at Premier Inn, 2A Queen's Road, Belfast, BT3 9DT.

Staying in Central Belfast

Staying in Belfast's city center means you'll be close to much of the city's action, making it easy to get to other areas in the city. If you happen to be traveling to Belfast in December, you'll find yourself close to the Belfast Christmas Market, which is perfect for picking up any last-minute gifts for friends or family! Here are some of the hotels worth checking out in central Belfast:

The Fitzwilliam: The Fitzwilliam is a five-star luxury hotel with beautiful rooms to accommodate you after a long day of exploring Belfast. This hotel is next to the Grand Opera House and within walking distance of other major attractions near the city center.

Europa Hotel: Europa Hotel is a mid-range hotel famous for being bombed a record 36 times during the Troubles. This hotel offers traditional Irish hospitality and traditional rooms for your stay.

Holiday Inn Belfast City Center: The Holiday Inn Belfast City Center hotel offers mid-range accommodations in newly-refurbished rooms. This hotel is excellent for traveling with a family, as they offer family rooms.

Staying in the Cathedral Quarter

Ramada Encore: If you're looking for budget-friendly accommodation, the Ramada Encore is an excellent option. This hotel is steps from St. Anne's Cathedral and many other spots worth exploring in the Cathedral Quarter.

The Merchant: The Merchant is one of the most renowned luxury hotels in Belfast, dating back to the 1860s. This hotel is decorated with original artwork, stunning marble bathrooms, and more. After a long day of exploring, you can take advantage of their rooftop hot tub while enjoying the view of Belfast.

Malmaison: Malmaison is a boutique hotel set in a converted warehouse, making its interior attractive as the furnishings draw on its former life. This hotel is a short walk away from St. Anne's Cathedral and the Titanic Quarter.

What NOT to Do in Belfast

There are many reasons why people love to visit Belfast, but it's well worth taking in these three tips to ensure you have a leisurely few days in this famous Northern Ireland city!

Don't Overlook Attractions beyond the City Center
While Belfast's city center has much to offer, don't overlook attractions in the surrounding areas, such as the Giant's Causeway, Carrick-a-Rede Rope Bridge, and the Mourne Mountains. Plan your itinerary to include both city and countryside experiences.

Don't Skip the Peace Wall Tour
Belfast has famous Peace Walls that separate nationalist and unionist communities. Consider taking a guided tour to gain insight into the city's history and the peace process. Avoid making assumptions about the political situation without understanding its complexities.

Don't Skip checking for Events and Festivals.
Belfast hosts various events and festivals throughout the year. Check the calendar for cultural festivals, music events, and local celebrations that may align with your travel dates.

Don't Skip Visiting Street Art in the Cathedral Quarter

The Cathedral Quarter is known for its vibrant street art scene. Take the time to explore the area and appreciate the murals, which often reflect Belfast's history, culture, and political themes.

Don't Drive in Bus Lanes
If you rent a car, Belfast has bus-specific lanes, which you want to avoid getting caught driving in! Not only will you get fined, but you'll also frustrate the bus drivers!

Don't Worry About Taking Public Transportation
If you're okay with walking, you don't need to take public transportation everywhere! The city is small enough that you can get to the major attractions on foot. Plus, you'll be able to explore and see more by walking around!

Don't Expect to Find Easy Parking
Finding a parking spot in Belfast can be tricky! If you find a parking garage, park there and walk around instead because chances are, you won't find parking at every single place you're going to!

Belfast is a city worth checking out with its unique history, culture, arts, and entertainment. There is much to see and do, from exploring the Crumlin Gaol to learning more about the RMS Titanic. If you're looking for more adventure, we will return to the Republic of Ireland and explore County Cork, the second-largest city in Ireland.

Chapter 5:

Cork City—Dos and Don'ts

C ork is where many filmmakers venture to film their movies, thanks to its vast hills, seaside, landscapes, and mountains that make the area so unique. Some would argue that had Cork not existed, the backdrop for various blockbusters would not have been possible, most notably Star Wars VIII—The Last Jedi, which had a scene shot in Cork. There was something so perfect about the moody skies and the roaring sound of the Atlantic Ocean crashing into the cliffs that the crew knew this would be the ideal location for Luke's island.

Although Star Wars is one of the most notable movies to be filmed in Cork, there is so much more to the city, fused with its roots to the modern life it is today. This city is home to some brilliant contemporary art on display in historic buildings, beautiful beaches around the county, and fun and unique markets to explore within the neighborhoods! Let's dive further into some things you should do while in Cork.

What to DO in Cork City

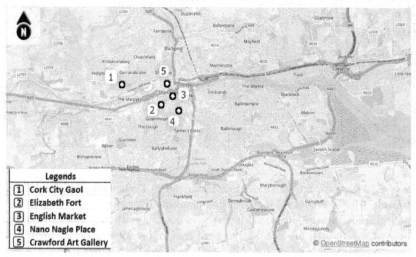

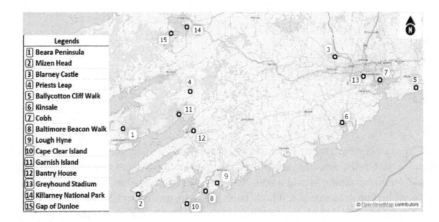

Legends
1. Beara Peninsula
2. Mizen Head
3. Blarney Castle
4. Priests Leap
5. Ballycotton Cliff Walk
6. Kinsale
7. Cobh
8. Baltimore Beacon Walk
9. Lough Hyne
10. Cape Clear Island
11. Garnish Island
12. Bantry House
13. Greyhound Stadium
14. Killarney National Park
15. Gap of Dunloe

With Cork being the Republic of Ireland's largest county and second-biggest city, it's also one of the most scenic places to explore. There are so many places you can visit while you're here! So, without overwhelming you with all the endless things you could do here, we'll look at the top highlights to explore while you're in Cork.

The Beara Peninsula

If you're looking for an entire outdoor excursion in Cork, venture to The Beara Peninsula. This peninsula is between the Kenmare River and Bantry Bay, and its beautiful landscape will likely stick with you even when you return home. This area is best to be explored on foot, but you can also follow some cycling routes. The cycling routes, which span 114 miles, will take you through all of the Beara Peninsula and its small coastal towns and villages along the way. The cycling routes are Glengarriff to Adrigole (14 miles), Adrigole to Castletownbere (11 miles), Bere Island (12 miles), Eyeries to Tuosist (30 miles) and Tuosist to Glengarriff and Spur to Kenmare (this is where you'll essentially hit a fork in the road to go in either direction and is 21 miles)

As for walking along the peninsula, you'll be rewarded with many archeological and historical sites on your journey. However, if you plan to be in Cork for at least a week, Caha Mountains and Slieve Miskish is a fantastic place to hike around Beara following the Beara Way Trail.

Mizen Head

Mizen Head doesn't have a specific address. If you're using Google Maps, it's best to search for their area code to get you there: P81 NY52.

Hours of operation: 1) November to March, it is open on weekends only from 11 a.m. to 4 p.m. 2) April, May, September, and October from 10:30 a.m. to 5 p.m. daily 3) June to August from 10 a.m. to 6 p.m. daily

The cliffs around Mizen Head are a hazard to ships, and it was becoming an apparent problem when ships were coming too far inland, causing them to sink and kill those on board. After the SS Stephen Whitney sank in 1847, a lighthouse was constructed to stand upon the Fastnet Rock to warn ships if they were too far inland. However, in 1906, the Irish Lights Board decided a fog signal was also needed for ships, so a fog signal station was built on Cloghane Island in Mizen Head to establish poor visual conditions for the sailors. Explosives would be used at three-minute intervals to warn ships that the sharp rocks and cliffs were nearby. Eventually, that became automated in the 1930s before the facility became a maritime museum in the 1990s. The museum has plenty of exhibits showcasing Mizen Head's history, an automatic weathering station, and a small-scale version of the original Fastnet Rock Lighthouse.

After you wander through the museum, wander down toward the newer signal station and walk across the arched bridge, where you might be lucky enough to see seals, dolphins, blue whales, or humpback whales below.

Individual Prices

Ticket type	Price
Adult	€ 7.50
Student/Senior	€ 6
Child under 14	€ 4.50
Child under five	Free
Family (two adults and up to four children)	€ 25

Group and Family Prices (Groups of 10 and up)

Ticket type	Price
Adult	€ 6.50
Student/Senior	€ 5
Child under 14	€ 3.50
Child under 5	Free

Cork Beaches

Since Cork is along the Wild Atlantic Way, if you're there in the summer, checking out one or a few of their beaches is a must! Here are some of the best beaches to check out:

Fountainstown Beach: Fountainstown Beach is 27 minutes outside Cork and is one of the more popular beaches to visit, especially if you're traveling with kids. There are two beaches in this area, which are about 700 meters apart. The front beach is much sandier and closer to the village, so it tends to be busier. On the other hand, the back beach has shallower waters, which is suitable for kids and is a bit quieter.

Myrtleville Beach: If you're looking for a place to see some seals from a distance, check out Myrtleville Beach. It's 29 minutes from Cork and is less crowded. One thing to note is that there isn't a car park at this beach, but you can park on the side of the road on the way to the beach.

Garryvoe Beach: Garryvoe is a sleepy village 35 minutes from Cork. The beach is a mix of sand and pebbles, making it fun for kids who love beach combing. There is also a playground nearby; if you're there in the summer, it is lifeguarded.

Garrylucas Beach: Garrylucas Beach is a hidden gem next to the Old Head of Kinsdale and the Kilconman Marsh. This is one of the beaches where you'll find beautiful white sand, grassy dunes, and rocky cliffs surrounding the beach. Garrylucas Beach is about 38 minutes from Cork.

Blarney Castle

Address: Monacnapa, Blarney, County Cork
Hours of operation: 9 a.m. to 4 p.m. daily

Blarney Castle is a medieval castle dating back to the 1200s; however, the original stone fortification was destroyed and rebuilt by Cormac Láidir MacCarthy, the King of Munster, in 1446.

The castle you will see is referred to as a tower house—but it's enormous compared to typical tower houses, which are traditionally no higher than five stories and have up to two main chambers with several ancillary rooms on each level. However, in the case of the Blarney Castle, there are two towers (the second one was added sometime in the 1500s), and you can see where the two phases meet on the north elevation.

Nonetheless, Blarney Castle has seen its years of battles and triumphs—most notably in 1646 when English Parliamentarian forces besieged it before being given to Donough MacCarty, the new Earl of Clancarty.

Although most travel to Blarney Castle to see the famous stone and kiss it, plenty of rich history is discovered within the castle walls—though the castle has more remnants than a full fortress today. The gardens, specifically the poison garden, are also a significant highlight at Blarney Castle. There are warnings before you enter, and for good reason: some deadly plants, including Wolfsbane, Mandrake, Hellebore, Nightshade, and Hemlock, can harm anyone. Tickets to Blarney Castle can be purchased online through their website.

Ticket type	Price
Adult	€ 20
Student (17 years old)/Senior (65 and up)	€ 16
Child (6 to 16 years old)	€ 9
Child (under six)	Free
Family (two adults and two children)	€ 50

Priest's Leap

If you're looking for another excursion off the beaten path in Cork, check out Priest's Leap. The legend behind the name tells the tale of a priest who was going to visit a sick person. He traveled anonymously but was told by a peasant he had been sold out and had soldiers in pursuit of him. The peasant offered the horse to the priest to try and escape the soldiers, but they caught up with him. Miraculously, the priest and horse managed to get away, making a gigantic leap across a canyon near the town of Bantry. The most interesting part about this tale is that the rock the horse and priest landed on allegedly turned to clay, capturing an imprint of the hooves and fingers of the priest, which you can see. So, was it a legend, or was it a true story? That's for you to decide.

As for going to this area, the Priest's Leap will take you through a narrow mountain pass that connects Coomhola Bridge to the village of Bonane. As a fair warning, much of the drive is a single lane, but you can walk or cycle it. Whichever way you experience Priest's Leap, the beautiful views give unparalleled scenes from Bantry Bay to the Caha Mountains!

The Ballycotton Cliff Walk

The Ballycotton Cliff Walk in East Cork is a treat to spend about 2 to 2.5 hours walking along (depending on your pace). This walk is 4.3 miles in total, and you will see some picturesque views along the way, including the Ballycotton Lighthouse, beaches, and wildlife. The lighthouse was constructed sometime in the late 1840s to early 1850s after a ship named Sirius sank, killing 20 sailors.

Kinsale

Kinsale is a lovely little fishing village about 14 miles from Cork that will make for a perfect weekend stop in your travels. This town is picturesque, with it being along the waterfront. Sprinkled with colorful buildings along the narrow winding streets, there are plenty of art galleries to check out and much more.

If you're looking for light outdoor excursions, check out the Scilly Walk and the Old Head of Kinsale Walk, which are about four miles long. The Scilly Walk will take you from the town to the famous Charles Fort, a late 17th-century star-shaped fort. If you decide to walk the Old Head of Kinsale Walk, this walk will take you to a point that juts out into the Atlantic Ocean about a hundred feet above sea level.

Suppose you're looking for other things to explore while here, the James Fort was built in the early seventeenth century. It's less preserved than the Charles Fort, but you'll find some other neat town views from here since it's right across from the harbor!

Cobh

Cobh (pronounced Cove) is another town on the east side of Cork. One of the first things you'll notice when you arrive in this waterfront town is the tall Cobh Cathedral standing tall above the harbor. From the cathedral, make your way down the Deck of Cards, two different streets adorned with colorful houses along the way that look like a deck of cards stacked up against one another.

Cobh was also the final port that Titanic stopped in. You can follow the Titanic Trail, which will bring you to the Queenstown Story Heritage Center to learn more. In addition, there is a memorial for the Lusitania, another White Star Line ship that sank nearby.

For other historical interests, you can board a ferry that will take you to Spike Island, which was once a sixth-century monastery, where you can learn all about the monks, monasteries, rioters, captains, and convicts to step foot in the 24-acre fortress.

The Baltimore Beacon Walk

The Baltimore Beacon's history stems from over 200 years ago after the famous Irish Rebellion of 1798. When the rebellion ended, the British decided that beacons and lighthouses should be constructed along the coastline as part of a warning system for the people at sea.

Fun fact: Given how violent the water can be around Ireland, you can sometimes see old shipwrecks, so you can understand why having markers is important!

The Baltimore Beacon you'll see on your walk was a replacement built in 1849—the original one fell into disrepair. It's an impressive 50 feet high that sailors can't miss! Walking toward it, you will find yourself walking along ancient stone walls from the 800-year-old Dùn na Séad to lead you there. It shouldn't take any more than 25 minutes to reach the beacon. While you're there, take some time to sit and enjoy the views of the Atlantic Ocean—you might even be lucky enough to see some whales jumping and splashing in the water!

Killarney National Park

Address: Killarney House & Gardens, Killarney National Park, Muckross Road, Killarney, V93 HE3C

Did you know Killarney National Park was Ireland's first designated national park? It was first bought as a wedding gift for a wealthy American's daughter and then eventually gifted to Ireland in 1932!

But despite earning its title as the first national park in the country, Killarney National Park is tucked between lakes, waterfalls, mountains, and a native oak forest among the nineteenth-century Muckross House and Gardens.

The park's vast size is home to plenty of different wildlife, including deer, red deer, Irish hares, otters, and birds for those who love to spot animals. It's also one for outdoor enthusiasts, as you can follow plenty of walking and hiking trails, horseback riding, boat tours, canoeing, and kayaking.

You will also find plenty of ruins scattered throughout the 25,000-acre park and old bridges, including the Old Weir Bridge, an ancient stone bridge dating back to the sixteenth century. This bridge connects the three leading lakes in the park: Lough Leane, Muckross Lake, and Upper Lake. This bridge is accessible by walking, biking, or boat tour. The park is open 24 hours daily, and almost everything is free. The costs you will incur are for renting canoes, kayaks, or bikes or taking a boat tour.

Gap of Dunloe

Address: Dunloe Upper, Gap of Dunloe, Co. Kerry, Ireland

The Gap of Dunloe, located six miles west of Killarney National Park, is a breathtaking mountain pass between MacGillycuddy's Reeks range and Purple Mountain. What makes this gap truly remarkable is its ancient origin, dating back two million years, when it was formed by the slow ice movement between the two mountains.

Immerse yourself in the awe-inspiring beauty of the Gap of Dunloe by embarking on a scenic walk. Spanning eight miles, starting early is advisable to savor its incredible views fully. Alternatively, horseback riding is also available.

For rock climbing enthusiasts, the Gap of Dunloe is a paradise. It boasts some of the finest rock climbing routes, including the exhilarating challenges of Céim and Bothàn crags. If you're new to rock climbing, it's recommended to go with a guide to ensure your safety and enjoyment.

Lough Hyne

A seawater lake called Lough Hyne is nestled between the rolling hills just three miles outside of Skibbereen. Interestingly, it used to be a freshwater lake over

4,000 years ago. However, with the Atlantic saltwater flowing into Lough Hyne twice a day through Barloge Creek, it's changed its biology and helped the lake to create its ecosystem by converting the water to salt water and warming the lake up with oxygenated seawater to support the marine plants and fish that live there (72 species to be exact). As a result of the changes, it piqued the interest of scientists for years, eventually being designated as the first Marine Natural Reserve in Europe in 1981.

The best place to observe and appreciate the view of Lough Hyne is from Knockomagh Hill. You can get there by following the Lough Hyne walk. It's a trek with a steep climb to the top, but even people with moderate fitness levels can conquer the hill's summit. (Plus, there are plenty of places to stop and enjoy the views.)

Another neat thing to consider doing at Lough Hyne is after-dark kayaking, as the lake has a glow to it thanks to the bioluminescence. This excursion can be found through various tour companies, such as the Atlantic Sea Kayaking, which costs €75 per person.

Teardrop and Cape Clear Island

Cape Clear Island, the southernmost inhabited Gaeltacht island in Ireland, is home to 147 people. Despite its small size, there are numerous activities to enjoy. One of the highlights is taking a boat tour to observe migratory birds and other wildlife. Another option is to board a ferry to "Teardrop," where the Fastnet Lighthouse is located. Interestingly, the name "Teardrop" originated from its significance as the last sight locals saw when departing Ireland by boat, symbolizing an emotional journey toward a new life.

For those interested in learning more about the island, the Heritage Center is a must-visit. Housed in a former school for girls, it showcases various artifacts from the island's earlier years.

Cape Clear also hosts an annual International Storytelling Festival every September. This vibrant event features live performances, themed storytelling, and a variety of workshops to engage and entertain attendees.

Garnish Island

Hours of operation: 1) April, May, September, and October: 10 a.m. to 5:30 p.m. daily 2) June, July, and August: 10 a.m. to 5:30 p.m. from Sunday to Friday and 10 a.m. to 6 p.m. on Saturdays

The island is closed from November to March.

Garnish Island is in the small Glengarriff harbor, sometimes called Ilnacullin or Illaunacullin (Island of Holly). This island is a popular destination thanks to its charming and peaceful gardens, created by Harold Peto, an architect for John Annan Bryce, who purchased the island in 1910 from the War Office. When Bryce passed away in 1923, his wife, Violet, continued to develop the gardens, with their son, Rowland, eventually taking on the responsibility about ten years after Bryce's passing. Rowland enlisted the help of Scottish gardener Mudro MacKenzie and added more plants from around the world to the garden. When Rowland died in 1953, Garnish Island was given to the Irish Nation and maintained by the Office of Public Works, allowing visitors from afar to continue enjoying the garden's tranquil atmosphere.

Getting to the island is pretty easy as you have your selection of three different ferry services to get you there, all leaving from Glengarriff:

Blue Pool Ferry: The Blue Pool Ferry leaves from the Blue Pool Amenity next to the Quills Woolen Market in the center of Glenfarriff. The ferries depart every 30 minutes between April and October. Tickets are €10 per passenger.

Harbor Queen Ferry: The Harbor Queen Ferry departs from the main pier across from the Eccles Hotel every 30 minutes between April and October. Tickets are €12.50 per passenger.

Ellen's Rock Boat Service: This ferry service leaves from Ellen's Rock, a mile outside town. The departure times vary based on the number of people.

When you are on your way to Garnish Island, keep an eye out for Seal Island, home to the largest seal colony in the harbor. They're used to the boat traffic and will happily lap the sun on the rocks as your boat passes.

After departing the ferry, you'll want to check out the gardens (especially the walled garden comparable to a secret garden), but also take the time to take in the views from the Martello Tower (accessible via the gardens). This tower dates back to 1805.

There is an admission fee for the island (in addition to ferry prices) as well: Adults: €5, Children: €3, Families: €13

Things to Enjoy in Cork

You can explore and do plenty of things in Cork, but don't forget about the experiences encompassing your travels in this vibrant city!

Bantry House

Address: Bantry House, Bantry, County Cork
Operating months: Bantry House is only open from April 1 to October 30.

Experience the breathtaking beauty of Bantry House and Gardens, a historic estate in the heart of Cork. Immerse yourself in centuries of history as you explore this enchanting property that's been in the White family since 1730. Spanning across 60 acres of beautifully manicured gardens, Bantry House offers a captivating view of the picturesque Bantry Bay. Inside the house, you will be awed by the grandeur of the rooms and then wander through the lush and colorful gardens. The estate also doubles as a bed and breakfast if you're looking for a place to stay during their operating months. However, you don't need to stay here to discover its treasures, art collections, and antique furniture.

Cork City Gaol

Address: Convent Avenue, Sunday's Well, Cork City, T23 VX2

Hours of operation:

Between March and October: 10 a.m. to 5 p.m. daily

Between November and February: from 10 a.m. to 4 p.m.

The goal is closed from December 22 to December 26.

As Cork is steeped in rich history and has plenty of archaeological treasures to discover while on your travels, one of the most captivating sites in Cork is the Cork City Gaol. This impressive building nearly looks like a castle and was once the home to prisoners during the nineteenth century. Touring this jailhouse is unlike anything else—it might even leave you with goosebumps! The cells contain lifelike wax figures, making the jail feel alive. As you wander through the cells, take the time to admire the graffiti that reveals some of the deepest thoughts of the prisoners. In addition, an audio-visual show will teach you more about the different lifestyles and societal standards during the nineteenth century.

You can tour the jail by yourself or on a guided tour. If you want to join a guided tour, these tours are at 2 p.m. daily and run for about 45 minutes. Guided tours run every hour on the hour if you're going to the gaol during July or August. (Please note that guided tours are only available in English.)

All self-guided tours come with a guidebook in nine different languages.

Ticket type	Self Guided	Guided tour
Adult	€ 10	€ 12
Student/senior (65 and up) with valid ID	€ 8.50	€ 10.50
Child (3 to 17 years old)	€ 6	€ 8
Children under 3	Free	Free
Family ticket	€ 30	€ 32
Audio guides (additional cost)	€ 2	Not applicable

Tickets can be booked online at the Cork City Gaol website.

Jameson Distillery—Midleton Distillery Experience

If you didn't get a chance to check out the Jameson Distillery in Dublin, don't fear! There's one in Cork, too! Here are some of the experiences you can enjoy at this location.

Cask Opening Experience (€25 per person)

During the 30-minute cask opening experience, you will visit the whiskey maturation house and learn about the "Angel's Share" (Midleton Distillery Experience, n.d.). You'll also get to draw a Special Jameson Blended Whiskey (in addition to tasting it). Delicious!

Premium Whiskey Tasting (€32 per person)

Sit with a whiskey expert as you taste some of the premium whiskeys. The Jameson ambassador will take you through four different whiskeys, and you'll learn more about each one and how they differ.

Midleton Distillery Experience Tour (€26 per person)

Tour the original Midleton Distillery with one of Jameson Distillery's expert guides. On this 75-minute tour, you will watch a short film and learn about the people responsible for the various processes involved in making the seven different brands of the iconic Irish whiskey. In addition, this tour will take you through several important buildings, warehouses, and the Micro Distillery. At the end of the tour, you can enjoy a tasting of three popular whiskeys, including Jameson.

Midleton Distillery Experience and Premium Whiskey Tasting (€52 per person)

This Midleton Distillery experience is a one-up from the regular tour. You will still get to discover Jameson's heritage and learn about the innovations at the distillery while touring some of the key buildings; however, at the end of the tour, you will get to taste four whiskeys instead of three. This guided tour will last about two hours.

Midleton Cocktail Class (€55 per person)

The Midleton cocktail class is a one-hour whiskey cocktail-making class hosted by Jameson's mixology team. During this class, you'll learn how to make three different cocktails from start to finish (and enjoy them).

Behind the Scenes (€65 per person)

The behind-the-scenes experience is two hours long and will take you through a more extended tour of the distillery and the grounds, including the Micro Distillery, the Maturation Warehouse, the Cooperage, and the Distiller's Cottage. In addition to learning about the history, you'll also get to taste premium whiskeys throughout the tour.

Distiller's Apprentice Tour (€95 per person)

Take a rare experience and go behind the scenes during the Distiller's Apprentice Tour! This tour will give you access to Jameson's production and warehouse facilities, where you can learn about their processes, from distillation to maturation and all the other little steps needed to produce their whiskey. This tour is 2 hours and 45 minutes.

Discover Academy

€350 per person

Suppose you have a whole day where you want to learn about everything that goes into whiskey production; check out the Discover Academy excursion at the distillery. This experience goes from 10 a.m. to 4:30 p.m., and this interactive experience will bring you through the working distillery, have you sampling from the casks, and much more! Lunch is also included in this excursion.

Elizabeth Fort

Address: Elizabeth Fort, Barrack Street, Cork City, T12 C8AO

Hours of operation:

From October to April: 10 a.m. to 5 p.m., Tuesdays to Saturdays, and 12 p.m. to 5 p.m. on Sundays

From May to September: 10 a.m. to 5 p.m., Mondays to Saturdays, and 12 p.m. to 5 p.m. on Sundays

If the Elizabethan Era interests you, the Elizabeth Fort is worth spending an hour or so at. The star-shaped fort was built in 1601 during Queen Elizabeth I's reign in response to an ongoing war between the Old English and the Gaelic Irish. This fort was built to protect Cork from attacks while suppressing potential rebellions. It was taken down two years later, in 1603, because the people of Cork were worried the fort would be used against them by England. However, after Lord Mountjoy retook the fortification, the fort was rebuilt.

The fort had its fair share of uses over the centuries. During the Great Famine in the 1840s, it was a place to provide food. When the Irish War of Independence happened between January 1919 and July 1921, the British Army occupied the fort to fight the Irish Republican Army. It was even a police station from 1929 until 2013!

General admission to the Elizabeth Fort is free. However, if you want to take a guided tour, they happen at 1 p.m. daily and are €5 per person.

The English Market

Address: Grand Parade, Centre, Cork, Ireland

Hours of operation: Mondays to Saturdays from 8 a.m. to 6 p.m.

If you're looking for a fun market in Cork, you should check out the famous English Market. This market has been around since 1788, making it the oldest covered market in Europe. It survived many struggling moments, including famine, flood, war, fires, and recessions!

At this market, you will find a wide variety of locally sourced fresh produce, including fruits, vegetables, meats, seafood, cheeses, baked goods, and artisanal products, which is perfect if you're staying at a self-catering accommodation.

Nano Nagle Place

Address: South Presentation Centre Ltd., Douglas Street, Cork City, T12 X70A

Hours of operation: 10 a.m. to 5 p.m. daily

Nano Nagle Place is one of Cork's most historical sites. It was named after Nano Nagle, an Irish Catholic religious sister who wanted to provide free education to the poor and marginalized communities in Ireland during the eighteenth century— but building the school would not be an easy feat and had to be done in secret, or else she could face up to three months in prison due to the existing penal laws that restricted Catholic education.

The first school Nano Nagle established was on Cove Lane (now Douglas Street). She established several more institutions around Ireland, earning her the nickname the "Lady with the Lantern," as she often traveled at night and taught her pupils in secret.

Nano Nagle Place has been transformed into a beautiful heritage and education center. The buildings that had fallen into disrepair over the centuries have been restored, and new structures have been added to welcome you. You'll be able to explore the heritage museum, exhibition spaces, and beautiful gardens and learn how Nano Nangle Place continues to honor Nano Nagle's legacy by promoting education, social justice, and community engagement.

Ticket type	Self-guided tour	Guided tour
Adult	€ 7.50	€ 10
Student/Senior	€ 5	€ 6.50
Child (4 to 12 years old)	€ 4.50	€ 4.50
Child (under four)	Free	Free
Family	€ 18	€ 18

Crawford Art Gallery

Address: Emmett Place, Cork, T12 TNE6
Hours of operation: 1) Mondays, Tuesdays, Wednesdays, Fridays, and Sundays: 10 a.m. to 5 p.m. 2) Thursdays: 10 a.m. to 8 p.m. 3) Sundays and bank holidays: 11 a.m. to 4 p.m.

The Crawford Gallery, founded by William Crawford, a noteworthy Cork businessman and art collector, is another of Cork's most important historical buildings dating back to the early eighteenth century. The gallery is home to a diverse collection of paintings, sculptures, drawings, and prints from the eighteenth century to contemporary video installations. The gallery also houses beautiful Greek and Roman sculpture casts brought to Cork from the Vatican Museum in Rome in 1818.

In addition to its permanent collection, the Crawford Gallery hosts temporary exhibits throughout the year to showcase contemporary artists, making the gallery integral to promoting the arts in Cork. There is no admission fee for the Crawford Gallery.

Greyhound Stadium

Address: Bishopstown Road, Curraheen, Co. Cork T12 HNP4
Have a fun night at the Greyhound Stadium, where you can watch greyhounds racing! The atmosphere is fun, even if you're not a seasoned racegoer!

Race nights happen every Friday and Saturday at 7:35 p.m. (doors open at 6:30 p.m.).

Ticket type	Price
Classic combo* (minimum of two tickets)	€ 15
Adult general admission	€ 10
Student/Senior/Child general admission	€ 5

*All admissions give you a race program. However, if you go with the classic combo, you will also get a €3 tote betting voucher, a beverage of choice, and access to the ground floor and outdoor grandstand areas.

Must try food in Cork City

Spiced Beef: Cork is famous for its spiced beef, especially during the Christmas season. It's a flavorful, aromatic beef dish that's been marinated in a mix of spices, including juniper, cloves, and allspice. The beef is slowly cooked, resulting in a tender and tasty delicacy. Spiced beef is often served cold, thinly sliced, and accompanied by pickles and mustard.

Beamish Stout Pie: Cork is home to Murphy's and Beamish, two renowned stout

breweries. The rich, velvety stouts produced by these breweries are often used in cooking. One popular dish is the Murphy's or Beamish Stout Pie, where tender pieces of beef or lamb are slow-cooked in stout, creating a hearty and flavorful filling for a savory pie. This dish is the epitome of comfort food.

Cork Buttered Salmon: Cork is located near the Atlantic Ocean, providing

access to fresh seafood. Cork Buttered Salmon is a local delicacy where fresh salmon fillets are pan-fried to perfection and served with a rich, creamy sauce made with locally produced butter. The combination of the tender salmon and the indulgent butter sauce makes for a delightful and luxurious meal.

Drisheen: Drisheen is a traditional Irish blood pudding that is a specialty in Cork.

It's made using sheep's blood, fat, and a binding agent such as oatmeal or breadcrumbs. The mixture is seasoned and then boiled or steamed to create a firm, sliceable pudding. Drisheen is often served fried, accompanied by bacon or sausages, and is a unique dish to try for those looking to explore local flavors.

Cork-Style Dry Cure Bacon: Cork-style dry cure bacon is a beloved local

specialty. Pork belly or loin is dry-cured with a mix of salt, sugar, and spices, resulting in a flavorful and slightly salty bacon. It's typically sliced thickly and pan-fried until crispy. Cork-style dry cure bacon is a key component of traditional Irish breakfasts and is enjoyed with eggs, sausages, and other breakfast items.

Where to Stay in Cork

Although Cork is the second largest city in the Republic of Ireland, there are plenty of places to stay within and outside the city limits—it all depends on what you plan to do in Cork and how many people you travel with. This section will highlight some top neighborhoods and accommodations to consider in Cork.

Staying in Blarney

Blarney is famous for its castle and gardens, but because it's a suburb of Cork, it also makes for quiet nights when the city starts to sleep. In addition, there is good public transportation in Blarney, so you don't even need to worry about having a car if you want to go to the city center for the day. Here are some great options to stay in:

Muskerry Arms: The Muskerry Arms is a budget-friendly accommodation close to Blarney Castle. The hotel has a restaurant that offers homemade food on its menu.

Blarney Castle Hotel: The Blarney Castle Hotel is popular for people traveling with their families. The hotel is set in a building dating back to 1837. You can expect the rates of the rooms to be in the mid to higher range.

Staying in Cork City Center

If you want to be right in the city's heart, staying in Cork's City Center is a good option as it will put you closer to the other areas you plan to visit. This is a good option if you're a solo or couple traveling through Ireland or if you're only going to be in Cork for a weekend.

Jurys Inn Cork: Jurys Inn is an affordable accommodation, making it perfect for traveling with families. This hotel is close to the English Market.

Maldron Hotel South Cork City: The Maldron Hotel South Cork City hotel is in the center of Cork City, putting you right near several of the popular attractions; however, it's also close to public transportation to visit other areas of Cork. Prices are in the mid to high range and fluctuate based on the season.

Imperial Hotel Cork City: Feel like royalty when you stay at the four-star Imperial Hotel Cork City! This luxury hotel is in the heart of Cork and offers spa services, and some of the rooms have balconies that overlook the city skyline.

Staying in the Victorian Quarter

The Victorian Quarter is famous for the number of Victorian buildings in the area. It's located north of Cork's city center along the River Lee and has plenty of accommodations that fit travelers on a budget or if you're looking for luxury.

Sheila's Cork Hostel: If you're a solo traveler, check out Sheila's Cork Hostel. This hostel is near the city center, the English Market, and Cork City Gaol. This hostel can accommodate families but requires advance contact as visitors under 18 cannot stay in the shared dorm rooms.

Gabriel House Guesthouse: Gabriel House Guesthouse is a house dating back to the 1900s. It overlooks the harbor and Cork's cathedral spires and is near the Nano Nagle Place and Blarney Castle. The hotel offers a traditional Irish breakfast made with fresh eggs and ingredients.

The Montenotte Hotel: The Montenotte Hotel is a beautiful luxury hotel setting you a mile outside Cork's city center. This hotel has beautiful views of the city for relaxing in the evening and an in-house cinema if you're looking to watch a movie!

If you're looking for self-catering accommodation, check out Airbnb to see what is also available!

What NOT to Do in Cork

Don't Explore these areas in Cork City
If you're out at night, there are a few areas to avoid if you're walking and concerned about your safety. 1) The north side of Cork: Cork's north side is known for being rough around the edges. Please stick to the Victorian Quarter around MacCurtain Street. 2) Lee Walkway: The Banks of the Lee Walkway are gorgeous during the day but are very dark and secluded at night.

Don't Omit Taking a Day Trip to Kinsale

Kinsale, a picturesque town near Cork, is known for its colorful streets and excellent seafood. Don't Skip a day trip to explore its charm.

Don't Underestimate Cork City Steep Hills
Cork has some steep hills. Avoid wearing uncomfortable footwear, and be prepared for a bit of uphill walking when exploring different parts of the city.

Cork is undoubtedly a beautiful city to explore, with its breathtaking natural landscapes and rich history—you can see why filmmakers love to come here! Whatever you decide to do in Cork, you'll want to return soon!

In the next chapter, we will return to Northern Ireland to explore some of the best places to visit and activities to enjoy. There is so much to see and do in this part of the country!

Chapter 6:

Northern Ireland—Dos and Don'ts

O ne of Northern Ireland's claims to fame is that it is home to actor Liam Neeson. Neeson has an accolade of movies under his belt, most notably being the leading actor in Spielberg's 1993 film Schindler's List and Curtis's 2003 film Love Actually. He was also the voice of Aslan in The Chronicles of Narnia films directed by Adamson (2005 and 2008) and Apted (2010).

At this point, we have looked at Belfast in Northern Ireland, but there are plenty of other places to explore in this United Kingdom country. Maybe it's the smell of the fresh, saltwater air or the beautiful landscapes. But beyond the fun and busyness of Belfast, there are plenty of other areas to explore!

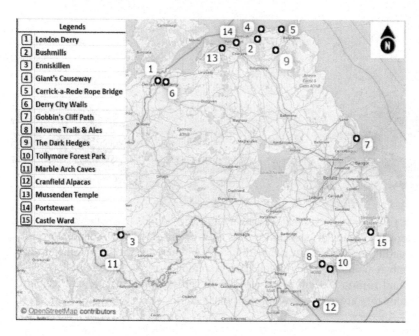

Every town in Northern Ireland brings a different atmosphere, especially if you're looking for some entertainment to enjoy as a night out, enjoying live music, or trying different drinks at their various breweries. If you're out in the country, some of Northern Ireland's rural areas give you some of the best stargazing sights—you may even be lucky to see the Northern Lights on a clear night!

Whatever will bring you to Northern Ireland, take advantage of some of the exciting things you can do beyond Belfast!

What to DO in Northern Ireland

There are plenty of options if you're looking for things to do in Northern Ireland outside of what we covered in the Belfast chapter! Belfast might be the "central" part of Northern Ireland, but beyond the city limits, there are plenty of places to explore and things to experience in this beautiful country! Let's get into it.

Derry-Londonderry

Have you ever stepped inside a walled city? This sounds like something out of a dystopian TV show or book, but it does exist if you go to Derry-Londonderry! It's an exciting and vibrant city rich with history and heritage within its walls. It's also the only remaining walled city left! Derry-Londonderry's walls were built between 1613 and 1618 to fend off early seventeenth settlers from England and Scotland, meaning they are over 400 years old today!

There are several gates which lead into the city. They are

Shipquay Gate: This is one of the original gates and was updated in 1805. However, the original gate had a tower and portcullis as it led into the city from the river.

Butcher Gate: Butcher Gate is another one of the original gates into Derry-Londonderry, but it was damaged during a siege in 1689 and rebuilt a little over 100 years later. The name came from Butcher's Street, where many butchers had shops.

Bishop's Gate: Bishop's Gate is an impressive triumphal arch installed in 1789 when the original gate was replaced. You can access the City Walls on either side of the gate.

Ferryquay Gate: The Ferryquay Gate overlooked River Foyle's ferryquay. When it was first constructed, it had a tower and a drawbridge. However, when it was replaced in 1865, those pieces were removed.

New Gate: New Gate was added to the City Walls in 1790.

Castle Gate: The Castle Gate was added between 1805 and 1808 below the Butcher Gate.

Magazine Gate: This gate was built in 1888 to allow more access to the riverfront from the city.

The best way to experience this small city is to walk the walls. One of the walks you can do is the dry moat walk, which will take you around the exterior of the Walled City through a dried moat. Along this walk, you will see three bastions on the platform that once protected the city from attacks: Church, Double, and Royal. To access this walk, you will want to exit through the New Gate, pass Bishop's Gate, and then come back into the city through Butcher Gate.

Another walk to check out while you're in Derry-Londonderry is to take a stroll on the ramparts top walk, an elevated walk that will take you above the city, allowing you to see the layout of the city. What is neat about this walk is that you'll see that the circumference of the walls is under a mile and shows the highest and lowest points of what was once the Island of Derry. You can access the ramparts to walk through Guildhall Square by taking the steps or ramp at Magazine Gate or the stairs at Bishop's Gate. The other option for accessing this walk is using Stable Lane.

Beyond walking the walls, check out the Craft Village if you're into crafts. It's in a tiny pocket of Derry-Londonderry in a reconstructed eighteenth-century street and nineteenth-century square. The doors to the buildings are colorful and house several independent businesses, from bookshops to crafts and cafés to small eateries.

One last thing to consider while in Derry-Londonderry is to take a walk across the Peace Bridge, which will bring you to Ebrington Square. This bridge was built in 2011 to symbolize Derry-Londonderry's new beginnings of being free from tension and conflict that affected the city for centuries.

Bushmills Village

Bushmills Village is a small town along the River Bush about 60 miles from Belfast in County Antrim. This village is best known for its namesake, the Old Bushmills Distillery, but many people venture this way as it brings them to the Giant's Causeway and the Carrick-a-Rede Rope Bridge. These two areas are worth exploring, which we will discuss in a moment, but this area is also popular because it is surrounded by picturesque countryside, perfect for taking photos and posting them on social media!

The Giant's Causeway

Address: 44 Causeway Road, Bushmills, County Antrim, BT57 8SU

Hours of operation: The Giant's Causeway's coastline is open from dawn until dusk. If you're driving or want to visit the visitor center, the hours are 10 a.m. to 6 p.m.

Explore the Giant's Causeway, one of the world's greatest natural wonders, which is a must-explore place to understand its significance! The Atlantic Ocean surrounds this area and offers some of the most striking scenes with its dramatic cliffs, including the stone columns left by volcanic eruptions over 60 million years ago! It is one of the most stunning views in Northern Ireland and not something to miss if you're up in this part of the island!

Visitor Experience (Nonpeak and Shoulder Season)

Ticket type	Price
Adult	£13.50
Child	£6.75
Family	£33.75
One adult family	£20.25

Visitors Experience Peak Season

Ticket type	Price
Adult	£15
Child	£7.50
Family	£37.50
One adult family	£22.50

If you plan to drive to the Giant's Causeway, parking is £10 on top of the admission fee.

Carrick-a-Rede

Address: 119a White Park Road, Ballintoy, County Antrim, BT54 6LS

Are you brave enough to walk across the rope bridge suspended across the Atlantic Ocean? If you are, the Carrick-a-Rede rope bridge connects Carrick Island to the County Antrim mainland, swaying 30 meters above the ocean!

Interestingly, the bridge has been around since 1755, when a salmon fisherman lived on the island. Don't worry if it's going to break. It's since been updated, so you'll be safe while walking across the 20-meter bridge! It will make for some fantastic photos and a different way to explore the landscape. The prices are the same as the Giant's Causeway entrance fees.

The Gobbins Cliff Path

Address: The Gobbins Visitor Centre, 68 Middle Road, Islandmagee, County Antrim, BT40 3SL

Like the Carrick-a-Rede Rope Bridge, the Gobbins Cliff Path is another dramatic and exciting excursion to explore in Northern Ireland, but it's more than simply exploring an outdoor area. The Gobbins Cliff Path is also an opportunity to explore a different time and immerse yourself in the elements.

When the Gobbins Path was constructed, it was the turning point of the twentieth century, and it was installed by Berkeley Deane Wise, who saw the potential in Northern Ireland's tourism industry with County Antrim as the dramatic backdrop combined with the growing railway system could bring more people here.

The Gobbins Cliff Path is only accessible on a guided tour, which runs for 2.5 hours. The tour will begin at Wise Eye's, a hole in a rock. As the Irish Sea waves crash beneath you, you'll continue to wander through narrow paths and up the stairs carved into the rock. You'll also be brought through tunnels beneath the sea! As you walk the path, you'll learn about the area's different biodiversity, see where puffins lay their eggs, and maybe even some dolphins splashing in the water. This is one of the most exciting things to do in Northern Ireland and should not be missed if you can go!

Ticket type	Price
Adult	£20
Child (up to 16)	£14.50
Student (with valid ID)/senior	£14.50
Family of three (two adults and one child)	£42
Family of four (two adults and two children)	£42
Family of five (two adults and three children)	£42

Please note that running shoes are not permitted on the Gobbins Path Walk. You need sturdy walking boots or hiking shoes. You can rent them for an additional £5 if you don't have any. Children must also be a minimum of four feet tall.

Enniskillen

Enniskillen is a neat 400-year-old town on an island. Of course, this town is steeped in history like everywhere in Northern Ireland! As you explore the village, you will want to check out a few places, such as Enniskillen Castle, which dates back to the sixteenth century. It's now home to two museums, the Fermanagh County Museum and the Inniskillings Museum, where you can learn about Enniskillen's local history and military heritage.

People also enjoy this town because it's right along the banks of Lough Erne. If you'd like to do this on a summer holiday, there are plenty of boating and water sports opportunities!

As you walk through the town on a self-guided tour, take in some other notable buildings dotted throughout the town. If you pop into the Blakes of Hollow for a pint, you'll also see a door featured in Game of Thrones!

This tiny island town has so much to do and see, making it a perfect weekend getaway!

Mourne Trails and Ales Tour

Address: Main Street, Castlewellan, County Down, BT31 9DQ

The Mourne Trails and Ales tour takes you on an adventure through one of the most beautiful regions in Northern Ireland. This guided biking tour will take you through the stunning landscape of the Mourne Mountains in the Castlewellan Forest Park. You'll also get to explore the fantastic history of the Annesley Estate and its connections to some of the favored food and drink worldwide.

At the end of the tour, you'll visit the Whitewater Brewery, where you can taste a selection of local craft beers paired with delicious eats!

The packages for the bike tour include 1) a helmet, which must be worn at all times, 2) an accessories pack with a lock, tool, pump, and tube, 3) a support number in case you need assistance, and 4) a damage waiver.

Bike type	Price
Enduro bike (electric)	£74.50
Downhill mountain bike	£64.50
Mountain bike (electric)	£54.50
Mountain bike (standard)	£29.50 to 39.50
Mountain bike (junior electric)	£19.50
Trail bike (electric)	£34.50

The Dark Hedges

Address: Bregagh Road, Stranocum, County Antrim, BT53 8PX

Step into a fairytale-like forest at the Dark Hedges, a picturesque avenue of beech trees the Stuart family planted in the eighteenth century. The Stuart family built the trees to make an exciting feature for visitors approaching their entrance. However, the trees have grown over time and created a neat archway and tunnel-like effect over the road. It's an impressive sight, and when you see it, you'll understand why it's such a popular destination because of how magical and otherworldly the trees make this road feel. The Dark Hedges have also appeared in the Game of Thrones if you're looking to take photos of the various filming locations of the TV show!

Tollymore Forest Park

Address: Bryansford Road, Tollymore Park, Newcastle, County Down, BT33 0PR

Tollymore Forest Park is one of Northern Ireland's beautiful parks, spanning nearly 630 hectares at the bottom of the Mourne Mountains. This park is a paradise with many scenic trails to explore and hike, giving you a panoramic view of Newcastle's surrounding mountains and sea. This park was also a filming location for Game of Thrones!

Some other park features to check out while here include 1) taking a stroll along the Shimna River in the center of the park, 2) walking across the stone bridges dating back more than 200 years, 3) walking along Cedar Avenue inside the Barbican Gate 4) going to the Hermitage, a 12 by 8-foot room made with a mass of stones 5) visiting the Clanbrassil Barn dating back to 1757

If you are looking for other outdoor activities at Tollymore Forest Park, you can follow horse riding trails in the forests and camp there, too!

Things to Enjoy in Northern Ireland

Bushmills Distillery

Address: 2 Distillery Rd, Bushmills BT57 8XH

Hours of operation: Monday to Saturday from 10 a.m. to 4:45 p.m.

Bushmills Distillery is a well-known distillery in Northern Ireland, famous for producing whiskey since 1608, making it the oldest licensed distillery in the world!

There are plenty of experiences at this distillery where you will learn all about the whiskey traditions they've held onto and passed through the generations.

Distillery Tour

Take a tour of the Bushmills Distillery with one of the whiskey educators to learn how Bushmills make their whiskey. This tour will take you through the history of the distillery and the grain-to-grass processes. This tour is £15 per person and lasts about an hour.

Premium Tour and Tasting

Take your tour of the Bushmills Distillery up one level with the premium tour and tasting experience. You will still learn about everything Bushmills does to create their iconic whiskey and then sample five of their whiskeys. This tour is £50 per person and lasts about an hour.

Enjoy a Pint and Food at the Walled City Brewery

Address: 70 Ebrington Square, Derry-Londonderry

Hours of operation: 1) Wednesdays and Thursdays from 5 p.m. to 8 p.m., 2) Fridays and Saturdays from 1 p.m. to 3 p.m. and 5 p.m. to 9:30 p.m., 3) Sundays from 1 p.m. to 5 p.m.

The Walled City Brewery is a multi-award-winning brewery and restaurant located at the end of the Peace Bridge. It is a family-owned pub that has been around since May 2015. This is a great place to stop, have a pint, and eat some delicious food after a day of exploring. However, they also offer several experiences worth checking out too!

Tour and Tasting: From Grain to Glass

Join one of the Walled City Brewery's brewers on a 45-minute tour as they take you through the processes of creating the Walled City Brewery's craft beers with their locally sourced ingredients while learning about the Brewery's history. During this experience, you will get to taste their signature brews. This experience is open to adults 18 and over and is £15 per person.

Beer Masterclass

At the beer masterclass experience, you will learn about the world of beer during a 90-minute class. You will go through the years of making beer, going back to 9000 B.C.E., and then continue through Ancient Rome, the Prohibition era, and right to where beer making is today. You're going to learn too much about how beer has evolved and shaped, as well as pick up some brewing techniques in case making your own is something that you've wanted to do! This interactive class will teach you so much about the popular drink of choice and everything that goes into making it! This experience is £25 per person.

Bogside History Tour

Derry-Londonderry has quite a turbulent history for it being a small walled-in city! You can learn much about the city's history by talking to the locals. But if you want to learn more about the city's recent history during the Troubles era, you must join a Bogside History Tour. This tour will take you around the city to where some of the notable events happened. Tours happen at 11 a.m. and 1 p.m. daily, costing £10 per person.

Marble Arch Caves

Address: 43 Marlbank Road, Legnabrocky, Enniskillen, County Fermanagh, BT92 1EW

Hours of operation: 1) Visitor Center: 10 a.m. to 5 p.m. daily 2) Guided tours: 10 a.m. to 3:30 p.m daily

The Marble Arch Caves is a unique and fascinating destination for adventure-seekers and nature lovers. This stunning underground cave system has plenty of passages, chambers, and waterfalls, all formed over 350 million years ago by the various rivers! (Nature is so calm!)

You can take guided tours through the Marble Arch Caves, following the Yorkshire Ramblers 1935 exploratory route. You'll get to see amazing formations in the rock, including stalactites, stalagmites, and flowstones, while learning about the history and geology of the caves. You'll also get to see many still pools and feel the energy of the waters gurgling as they splash into a black abyss.

If you're not so sure about exploring the caves, there are outdoor experiences to check out, including seeing the landscape draping over the cave and other seasonal events throughout the year.

If you are going to take the guided tour through the cave, it is between 60 to 75 minutes. The temperature in the caves is cool all year round (about 50 °F), so ensure you wear a sweater and comfortable shoes.

Ticket type	Price
Adult	£15
Child (5 to 17 years old)	£7.50
Child (under four)	Free

Student (18 and up)/senior (65 and up)	£12
Family (two adults and two children)	£37.50
Family (two adults and three children)	£45

Cranfield Alpacas Experience

Address: 35-37 Cranfield Road, Kilkeel, County Down, BT34 4LJ

Have you ever wanted to spend time with a cuddly alpaca? These animals are some of the most friendliest animals on the planet! The Cranfield Alpacas experience will get you up close and personal with these adorable animals, allowing you to take them for walks or hang out in the field! This is a perfect experience for the whole family!

Beach Trek

Take the alpaca for a lovely stroll along the beach on the beach trek experience! This experience is 90 minutes long and will take you along some country lanes down to the beautiful beach. This experience is not suitable for kids who are under six.

Ticket type	Price
Adult/child	£25
Additional guest (extra child or accompanying adult)	£10
Family (two adults and two children with two alpacas)	£55

Field Walk

The field walk experience is 60 minutes long and great for all ages! This experience will allow you to take the alpacas around the paddocks in Cranfield's field while enjoying the beautiful views of the Mourne Mountains and Carlingford Lough.

Ticket type	Price
Field walk ticket	£25
Additional guest (extra child or accompanying adult)	£10

Alpaca Adventure Trail

Meet, greet, and feed the alpacas in an up-close experience! This is a great way to enjoy hanging out with alpacas in a relaxed setting as you get to learn more about them. This experience is 45 minutes and is excellent for those with disabilities or if you're traveling with a stroller.

Ticket type	Price
Adult/child	£7.50
Baby (one and under	Free
Family (two adults and two children)	£25

Mussenden Temple

Address: Mussenden Road, Coleraine, Northern Ireland, BT51 4RG

The Mussenden Temple, an eighteenth-century building perched on the edge of a cliff, overlooks the Atlantic Ocean. Constructed in 1785, it was intended to serve as the library for Augustus Hevey, the wealthy Earl of Bristol and Bishop of Derry-Londonderry. The purpose of the library was to house numerous significant religious manuscripts. Inspired by the Temple of Vista in Italy, the temple features a distinctive circular design.

You can access the temple through the Downhill Demesne grounds, a beautiful estate surrounded by beautiful gardens and the picturesque Downhill Beach. The Downhill House, built in 1770, is also worth exploring, even though it's in ruins.

The Mussenden Temple and the surrounding grounds are free to visit.

Postewart Strand and Barmouth Wildlife Reserve

Address: Portstewart Strand, Portstewart, County Londonderry, BT55 7PG

Postewart Strand is an exhilarating beach that stretches for two miles, boasting golden sands and pristine, sparkling waters. It's an ideal destination for thrilling water activities like swimming, surfing, or leisurely walks along the water's edge. Just a stone's throw away lies the Barmouth Wildlife Reserve, a haven of vibrant flora and fauna. Immerse yourself in the diverse wildlife and soak in the breathtaking views of the surrounding landscape.

Castle Ward: Game of Thrones' Winterfell Castle

Address: Downpatrick Road, Strangford, County Down, BT30 7BA

Hours of operation: 10 a.m. to 4 p.m. daily

Step into Castle Ward, a magnificent eighteenth-century mansion in County Down, is well-known for its setting in Game of Thrones as the Stark family's Winterfell home. The house was built in the 1760s and features interesting architecture combining Gothic and Palladian elements in a beautiful County Down landscape.

When you visit Castle Ward, you can explore the house and its beautiful interiors, which are filled with period furniture, paintings, and decorative arts. You can also check out the stunning library, state bedrooms, and the Gothic staircase. On a nice day, explore the beautifully landscaped gardens and parkland, including a lake and a sunken garden. There are also 19 miles of trails worth exploring by foot or on a bicycle.

Ticket type	Price
Adult	£13.20
Child	£6.60
Family (two adults and two children)	£33
Family (one adult and two children)	£19.80

Must try food in Northern Ireland

Armagh Bramley Apple Pie: Northern Ireland is famous for its Bramley

apples, and one of the best ways to enjoy them is in a traditional apple pie. Armagh Bramley apple pie features tart and tangy Bramley apples encased in a buttery, flaky pastry crust. It's often served warm with a scoop of vanilla ice cream or a dollop of fresh cream, creating a delightful dessert experience.

Giant's Causeway Honey Ice Cream: Northern Ireland is known for its high-

quality honey, and one delightful way to enjoy it is in ice cream. Giant's Causeway Honey Ice Cream is made with local honey, creating a creamy and slightly sweet dessert. Enjoy a scoop of this indulgent treat, especially during warmer months, to experience the unique taste of Northern Irish honey.

Pastie Supper: A pastie supper is a classic fast-food dish in Northern Ireland. It

 consists of a pastie, which is a deep-fried pastry filled with minced meat, onions, and spices. The pastie is often served with chips (French fries) and accompanied by various condiments like gravy, curry sauce, or mushy peas. It's a hearty and satisfying meal, perfect for a quick bite.

Where to Stay in Northern Ireland

There are many reasons to stay in Northern Ireland beyond Belfast because of the vast landscape and endless adventures you can take outdoors! There is so much to explore and do in the country with the mountains and lush forests; you'll have stories to tell for years after you go home!

Staying in Derry-Londonderry

It would be quite an experience to say you stayed in the oldest and last walled city! Here are some of the top picks to keep in Derry-Londonderry:

Maldron Hotel: The Maldron Hotel is a budget-friendly accommodation in the heart of Derry-Londonderry, putting you central to some of the popular parts of the city, including the Craft Village and Peacebridge. They also offer a buffet breakfast to start your day!

Elagh Cottages: Elagh Cottages is a 10-minute cab ride from Derry-Londonderry's city center. This accommodation is a good option if you're looking for a self-catering and budget-friendly apartment!

Staying in Bushmills Village

With Bushmills being a smaller town, you can expect it to be quieter, which will make for a great relaxing evening after you explore the area! Some of the best places to stay are

Rest-A-While: This accommodation is a family-run bed and breakfast by the Causeway Coast and the Bushmills Distillery. They offer bicycle rentals as well as breakfast.

The Bushmills Inn Hotel: The Bushmills Inn Hotel is a luxury hotel in town situated along the Giant's Causeway. The building was once a Coaching Inn in the 1600s and has since been transformed into the boutique hotel it is today! Breakfast is included in your room.

Staying in Enniskillen

Sometimes, staying on an island is fun—even for a quick weekend getaway! Here are some of the places to look into if you want to stay in Enniskillen:

Finn Lough Hideaway: Escape to the tranquil forest and lake at the Finn Lough Hideaway! This accommodation is relaxing and unlike anywhere else you'd stay in Northern Ireland. The sites are beautiful; they offer yoga, have an outdoor fireplace, bike rentals, and canoeing.

Belmore Court and Motel: Belmore Court and Motel is a budget-friendly accommodation near the heart of Fermanagh and Enniskillen. People love this motel for its personalized service and its being near many shops and cafés.

Staying in Newcastle

Staying in Newcastle brings you closer to nature than ever, especially with this area being so close to the Mourne Mountains! This is a perfect spot for outdoor enthusiasts and nature enthusiasts alike. Therefore, if you want to check out some accommodations, look into staying at

Amble In B&B: Amble In B&B is a family-run accommodation, budget-friendly, and offers beautiful views of the mountains. All bedrooms are spacious and close to plenty of shops and restaurants in the area and the Royal County Down Golf Course (if you're looking to golf while in Ireland).

Slieve Donard Hotel: Step into luxury at the Slieve Donard Hotel, steeped in over 125 years of history. This stunning hotel is at the bottom of the Mourne Mountains and has some of the most exquisite rooms to relax in after exploring.

What NOT to Do in Northern Ireland

Don't Forget About Marching Season

Northern Ireland hosts an ancient tradition of celebrating William of Orange's victory during the Battle of the Boyne in 1690. Every year between June and July, the Orange Party (unionists) will take to the streets to march in celebration of this monumental part of Northern Ireland's history. While it is an exciting piece of history to remember, you'll want to verify when the march will happen if you want to avoid political rallies.

Don't Stay in Belfast the Whole Time

Although we have done an entire chapter on things to do in Belfast, given that this city is a part of Northern Ireland, it's important to note that you shouldn't feel the need to stick to the city. In this chapter, you have learned about the various places and things you should do in Northern Ireland, enhancing your overall trip to Northern Ireland!

Northern Ireland offers a lot to explore beyond the bustling city of Belfast, especially when you can experience spending time in a walled-in city, explore fairy-tale-like forests, and cuddle with some alpacas. This part of the United Kingdom has so much to offer, so ensure you choose the things that stand out the most to you to explore!

In the next chapter, we are going to check out the Wild Atlantic Way that runs along Ireland's west coast. This is one of the most scenic drives to do and has plenty of outdoor activities to do!

Chapter 7:

The Wild Atlantic Ways—Dos and Don'ts

T he Wild Atlantic Way is the longest coast drive in the world, spanning 1,500 miles of beautiful scenery and quaint Irish towns on the island's west side. This is the longest coastal route in the world, starting at Malin Head in County Donegal and leading you down to Kinsale in County Cork. Following this route will lead you through many towns you may not have thought to visit otherwise! Let's get right into what to do following the Wild Atlantic Way.

What to DO in the Wild Atlantic Way

There is so much excitement and adventure when you follow the Wild Atlantic Way, between exploring the towns dotted along the coast and enjoying live music in a pub. Some say following the Wild Atlantic Way is one of the best ways to experience the authentic life of the Irish while taking an adventure unlike anything else. This coastline will surely leave an impression on you!

The Towns of the Wild Atlantic Way

There are plenty of towns to explore along the wild Atlantic Way! However, to simplify it and avoid overwhelming you, let's check out the top towns to explore while making your way along the Wild Atlantic Way.

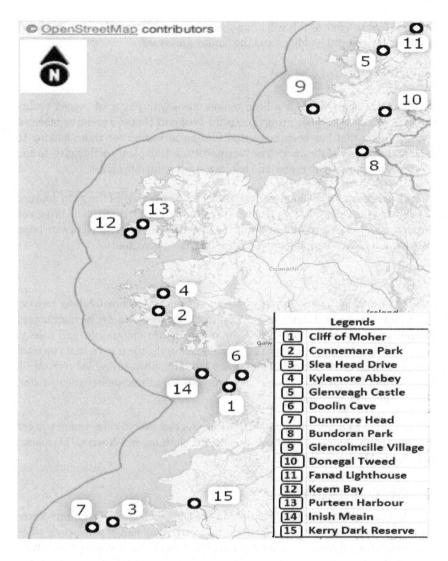

© OpenStreetMap contributors

Legends	
1	Cliff of Moher
2	Connemara Park
3	Slea Head Drive
4	Kylemore Abbey
5	Glenveagh Castle
6	Doolin Cave
7	Dunmore Head
8	Bundoran Park
9	Glencolmcille Village
10	Donegal Tweed
11	Fanad Lighthouse
12	Keem Bay
13	Purteen Harbour
14	Inish Meain
15	Kerry Dark Reserve

Donegal Town, County Donegal

Donegal Town is rich with beauty as it's surrounded by the Blue Stack Mountains, a 2.5-mile river, and lakes, with dramatic cliff-top views overlooking the Atlantic Ocean. Beyond its beautiful landscapes and views, Donegal Town is steeped in history dating back to the fifteenth century. This is the town where you can explore the ruins of the Franciscan Friary and the Donegal Castle. It's best to explore

Donegal Town on foot as this will bring you to many other notable areas, including admiring the colorful buildings and the famine graveyard.

Westport, County Mayo

Westport in County Mayo is a little remote town with plenty of rugged beauty throughout. One of its main attractions is the Westport House, a grand eighteenth-century home that has been converted into an attraction for those looking to explore the history of Westport. The Westport House has plenty of things to do and see, including an activity center and taking a stroll around the lakes.

This town is great for outdoor enthusiasts as there are plenty of things to do, such as following the Great Western Greenway, a 26-mile cycle path that will bring you through some of Westport's beautiful countryside. You'll pass plenty of bogs, villages, and coastline mountains while cycling along here, too!

Clifden, County Galway

Visiting Clifden in County Galway is a treat, surrounded by breathtaking views of the Atlantic Ocean and much more! This town has plenty to do, no matter your budget. There are shops to peruse if you're looking for unique gifts and pubs to enjoy a pint and some delicious eats. Clifden is also the town to be in if you want to experience great live music, as they host a Traditional Music Festival every April! This exciting festival also has a busking competition, a three-mile (five-kilometer) walk or run, and much more!

In addition to its lively music scene, there is a market every Friday where you can purchase fresh produce, homemade bread, pies, clothing, and flowers. This market happens in Market Square near the harbor.

Dingle, County Kerry

The charming town of Dingle is located in the Dingle Peninsula in County Kerry. This town is popular because of its beautiful scenery, bohemian and artistic vibes, and overall friendly and lively atmosphere. Plus, it's famous for being a Star Wars shooting location!

While in Dingle, you should check out the Slea Head Drive (more on that soon) and pay a visit to the harbor where you can see the bronze sculpture of Dingle's famous bottlenose dolphin, Fungie, who used to swim alongside the boats playfully. Although he's since passed away if you want to take a sea adventure to look for these playful mammals, check out the Dingle Dolphin Tours and the Dingle Sea Safari!

Killarney, County Kerry

Situated along the edge of the Killarney National Park, Killarney is one of the most-loved towns in Ireland. Maybe it's because of its wildlife, or perhaps it's because of its scenery, but there are plenty of things to do in this town. This town also lives and breathes some of its original roots, including using horse-drawn carriages that will take you through the park and around town.

Within the town, you'll see plenty of charming buildings full of colors, lively pubs, and delicious restaurants serving traditional Irish food. In addition, the nearby Muckross House and Gardens are worth exploring as they take you back to the Victorian-era lifestyle.

Cliffs of Moher

Address: Cliffs of Moher Visitor Centre, Lislorkan North, Liscannor, County Clare, V95 KN9T

Hours of operation: 1) March and April from 8 a.m. to 7 p.m. 2) May to August from 8 p.m. to 9 p.m. 3) September and October from 8 a.m. to 7 p.m. 4) November to February from 9 a.m. to 5 p.m.

The Cliffs of Moher are one of the most dramatic landscapes you will ever set your eyes on. These stunning cliffs are 214 meters above the Atlantic Ocean and give you some of the most spectacular coastline views as you listen to the ocean crashing into the cliffs below.

The visitor center is also worth checking out. It's set on a hill (like a hobbit house) and has an interactive exhibit that gives you the story of the cliffs, its geology, and

wildlife while integrating stories from around Ireland and County Clare. The display will teach you about climbing change, how the rocks and cliffs formed, and more!

While hanging around the cliffs, it might be a good idea to pack lunch and binoculars and enjoy a bite as you bird watch for puffins and other sea birds. If you're here in the evening, watching the sunset will grant you beautiful sky colors, perfect for taking photos and posting them on social media!

While at the cliffs, be sure to check out the O'Brien Tower. This tower was built by Sir Cornelius O'Brien in 1835 as an observation area for English tourists coming through County Clare. If the day is clear, you can see the Twelve Bens of Connemara and Aran Islands across from Galway Bay.

Be sure that you are prepared for the temperatures by the cliffs, as it can be quite windy and cool with the mist coming from the ocean.

The price to visit the Cliffs of Moher Experience in the visitor center is €7 per person. Children 12 and under are free, but there is a maximum of four children per adult booking. In addition to the interactive cliffs experience, your admission will give you access to all areas, including O'Brien's Tower.

Connemara National Park

Address: Letterfrack, Co. Galway, Ireland

Connemara National Park is a smaller version of the stunning landscapes that define Connemara. With its rugged mountains, lush green spaces, and captivating lakes, it attracts thousands of visitors each year. To truly immerse yourself in the raw beauty of Connemara National Park, a self-guided tour is highly recommended. This allows you to connect with nature at your own pace and choose trails that suit your fitness level. However, if you're afraid of getting lost, guided tours are also available.

While the park is home to various wildlife, it is renowned for its Connemara ponies, a unique breed found only in this region. These gentle giants with their speckled coats are a sight to behold. If ponies and horses don't pique your interest, watch for other wildlife and birds! For those seeking more outdoor adventures, camping in the park is worth considering.

Lastly, take advantage of the opportunity to explore the visitor center, which is free of charge. Here, you can delve into the fascinating history of Ireland's changing landscape since the ice age and enjoy a short film showcasing the ongoing work in Connemara.

Kylemore Abbey and Victorian Walled Garden

Address: Kylemore Abbey, Connemara, County Galway, Ireland, H91 VR90

Nestled near the edge of Connemara National Park is the Kylemore Abbey, a stunning Benedictine monastery dating back to the nineteenth century.

When it was built between 1863 and 1868, it was destined for the wealthy family of Michael Henry, an English politician from England who also served as an MP in County Galway between 1871 and 1885. After Henry's wife, Margaret, sadly passed away in 1875, he stopped visiting the exquisite home and eventually was sold to the Benedictine nuns who established the monastery in 1920. Shortly after, an international boarding school for girls was also opened, with many girls wanting to come to Kylemore Abbey due to Connemara's beautiful landscape. For many of those pupils, it also allowed them to learn English.

Due to maintenance costs and societal changes, Kylemore Abbey Boarding School saw the enrollment numbers decrease. By June 2010, the school was closed following examinations, but Kylemore does support education in other ways. The Notre Dame University in Indiana and Kylemore have exchange programs for students. In addition, Connemara's Maths Academy also uses the school rooms throughout the year. So, while it still sees classes, you can still tour the Abbey and immerse yourself in its long history.

The Victorian Walled Garden outside was built in the nineteenth century. At the time, it was a garden boasting fruits and vegetables for the estate. Today, the garden is home to a vast collection of other plants and flowers, some of which are rare and exotic.

To experience this beautiful mansion, booking your tickets online through their website is best.

Ticket type	Price
Adult	€ 16
Student (17 years old or with valid ID)/senior	€ 13.50
Junior student	€ 8
Family (two adults plus two to six children under 16)	€ 40
Child (12 years old and under)	Free

Slea Head Drive

Along the western tip of the Dingle Peninsula lies the breathtaking Slea Head circular drive, accessible from the town of Dingle. Brace yourself for an exhilarating 18-mile journey filled with stunning landscapes, rich history, charming Irish-speaking villages, iconic filming locations (including Star Wars), and awe-inspiring views of the mighty Atlantic Ocean. On a clear day, feast your eyes upon the magnificent Blasket Islands!

As you embark on this thrilling adventure, prepare to encounter numerous stops where you can immerse yourself in history. Explore ancient stone forts and marvel at the unique beehive-shaped huts crafted from stone!

One crucial tip: For an optimal experience, it is highly recommended to travel clockwise, especially during the summer when the road is frequented by large tour buses.

Glenveagh Castle

Address: Glenveagh National Park, Gartan Mountain, Church Hill, County Donegal, F92 HR77

Hours of operation: 1) 9:45 a.m. to 5:15 p.m. (the last tour is at 4:45 p.m.) 2) Please note that tours cannot be booked before you go to the castle.

Glenveagh Castle is a nineteenth-century castle nestled in the Glenveagh National Park. The castle was built by John George Adair, a wealthy landowner, between 1870 and 1873 as a hunting lodge destination.

Of course, when the castle was built, it was met with plenty of controversy, primarily because of the tenants being evicted from their homes for Adair to create his hunting estate. The evictions led to widespread outrage and condemnation, so it should be no surprise that Adair is still a name many Irish frown upon when asked about him.

Nonetheless, despite its dark and controversial history, this stunning castle has 32 rooms, many decorated with period furnishings, which is certainly something to explore. And, of course, with it being in another beautiful Irish national park, there are plenty of other outdoor things to explore and do!

You can explore Glenveagh Castle on a self-guided tour. The guided tour takes about 45 minutes and will take you through the main rooms of the estate as well as some of the bedrooms. In addition, you should check out the gardens, which you can do on your own or with a guided tour. These vibrant gardens have many beautiful plants and flowers blooming throughout the seasons.

Ticket type	Price
Adult	€ 7
Senior/student	€ 5
Family	€ 15
Children six and under	Free

Doolin Cave

Address: Craggycorradan West, Doolin, County Clare

Hours of operation: 10 a.m to 5 p.m. daily (the last tour is at 5 p.m.)

The Doolin Cave is a fully guided adventure that will take you 800 meters below ground. This stunning cave is home to the longest Stalactites in the world! It's so neat to see in real life, as it looks like a chandelier.

The tour will take you through the cave, and you'll learn more about the fascinating history of the cave dating back to over 350 million years ago, the geology of the cave and how it was formed, and see these amazing formations up close. You'll indeed feel like a great explorer when the tour ends!

After checking the cave out, walk along the eco-trail, accessible to everyone who adventures into the cave. This trail is under a mile long and will take you around the exterior of the cave setting, as well as seeing the original cave entrance.

As a forewarning, the tour involves climbing up and down 125 stairs and may not be suitable for those with mobility issues. Also, be mindful of the temperature as it is cool, no matter the season (52 °F), so you will want a light sweater or jacket. It's also advisable to wear sturdy, closed-toe shoes.

Prebooking your guided tour must be done through the Doolin Cave website. Tours start on the hour. If you are late, you cannot join.

Ticket type	Price
Adult	€ 18.50
Senior/Student	€ 16.60
Child (4 to 16 years old)	€ 9.50
Family of four (two adults and two children aged 4 to 16)	€ 52

Dunmore Head

Address: Dunquin, Dingle, County Kerry

Dunmore Head is located at Europe's furthest westerly point along the Dingle Peninsula. This is well worth coming to if you love hiking. The hike you can take will bring you to the highest point, where you'll find an Ogham stone. This stone is steeped with history and is one for archeologist enthusiasts as it has an ancient pagan script engraved. However, it also serves as a reminder of where the Spanish Armada ships sank to the bottom of the ocean in 1588.

After your hike, and if you're up for it, rent a bike and cycle around the surrounding countryside to discover and explore the nearby villages, well-loved for their friendly atmosphere! These villages are a great spot to stop for lunch, especially if you love seafood! Alternatively, picnic and watch the seabirds swooping down if the weather is great! You may even see a dolphin or another whale frolicking in the waters!

Things to Enjoy Along the Wild Atlantic Way

By now, you should know how great the Wild Atlantic Way is for adventuring enthusiasts! If the exploration isn't enough, let's look at other things you can do and enjoy along Ireland's famous west coast!

Bundoran Adventure Park

Address: Sea Rd, Drumacrin, Bundoran, County Donegal

Hours of operation: 1 p.m. to 10 p.m. during the summer months

It wouldn't be a seaside without a fun amusement park! The Bundoran Adventure Park is great for amusement park enthusiasts or for spending a few hours catching some thrills and making memories with your family! There are plenty of rides for any age, plus mini golf, bumper boats, bungee trampolines, go-karting, and games.

Park admission is free, but if you want to purchase wristbands, they must be done online. A Megaband gives unlimited access to the large, tiny tot rides and the bouncy castle. This band will also allow you to ride the Big Wheel once. The TinyTot bands will give your little ones two hours to ride on the TinyTot rides and the mini roller coaster and jump in the bouncy castle. Game stalls are cash only. Tickets are also available if you want to spend less than two hours at the park. These tickets come in a sheet of 25 and are only available at the park.

Ticket type	Price
Megaband	€ 19.95
TinyTot band	€ 14.95
Saver sheets tickets (25/sheet)	€ 20
Individual tokens	€ 1

The Big Wheel (Without the Megaband)

Ticket type	Price
Adult	€ 3.50
Child	€ 3
Child (under two years old)	€ 2
Family (two adults and two children)	€ 12

Adventure Golf

Ticket type	Price
Individual*	€ 4
Family of two	€ 7
Family of three	€ 10
Family of four	€ 13
Family of five	€ 15

*If you book online, it's €3 per person.

Other Attractions

Attraction type	Price (per five minutes)
Bungee trampolines	€ 4
Bumper boats	€ 3.50

Waterworld Bundoran

Address: Waterworld Bundoran, Atlantic Way, Bundoran, County Donegal

The Waterworld Bundoran is a fun indoor pool complex, perfect if the weather is not great for the beach! There are plenty of fun waterslides for all ages and a wave pool!

At the time of writing this book, this attraction is closed for the season and will reopen in the spring. Booking online and ahead is recommended. However, you can book tickets on the day of, so long as availability is due to the two-hour window. Pricing can also be found on their Facebook page.

Glencolmcille Folk Village

Address: Dooey, Glencolumbkille, County Donegal

Hours of operation: The Glencolmcille Folk Village is open from Easter until September 30 between 10 a.m. and 6 p.m. daily. Between October 1 and October 31, the village is open from 10 a.m. to 4:30 p.m. However, their website recommends you call them to confirm the exact closing nearing the end of the month as they may close sooner than October 31.

The Glencolmcille Folk Village is a living museum replicating traditional Irish culture and lifestyle in eighteenth, nineteenth, and twentieth-century rural Ireland. At this village, you'll immerse yourself in Irish heritage while exploring authentic thatched-roof cottages replicating life during the three respective centuries and the different eras of Irish history: a fisherman's cottage, a schoolhouse, and a pub-grocer.

You can explore everything on your own (or with a tour guide), interact with costumed actors who help bring the exhibits to life and learn about the customs, traditions, and daily routines of Irish people from the past. Alternatively, guided tours take you through the village, too.

If you're looking for a bite to eat, it's worth checking out the tea room, where you can enjoy homemade treats, including a guinea cake, apple tart, soup, sandwiches, and fruit or brown scones.

Ticket type	Price
Adult	€ 6.50
Student/Senior	€ 5.50
Children (seven and up)	€ 3
Children (under seven)	Free
Family (two adults and two children between seven and 14 years old)	€ 16.50
Three or more children	€1 per child
Groups (minimum of 11 people)	€ 5.50

Visit Eddie Doherty Donegal Tweed

Address: Front Street, Ardara, County Donegal, F94 XT95

 Although the art of hand-making traditional Donegal tweed is dying, one person in Donegal still makes this woven fabric by hand: Eddie Doherty. Doherty learned this craft when he was 16 and has been weaving Donegal tweed ever since, using traditional techniques and Donegal wool to create beautiful wool blankets and tweed—all by hand! While taking a gander around the shop, be sure to talk with Doherty, as he is always pleased to give visitors a demonstration of how he creates his beautiful tweed products using his handloom.

To find out the shop hours, stroll through the beautiful main street of Ardara.

Fanad Lighthouse

Address: Cionn Fhánada Eara Thíre na Binne, Baile Láir, County Donegal, F92 YC03

Hours of operation: Tuesday to Sunday from 11 a.m. to 4 p.m.

The Fanad Lighthouse has played an important role in Ireland's maritime history since its first lighting in 1817. Like the purpose of all lighthouses, it was constructed after HMS Saldanha, a Royal Navy frigate, hit rocks during a violent storm and sank on the night of December 4, 1811, killing all of her sailors except a parrot. Since the lighthouse's construction, it has continued to play an important role in keeping ships and their passengers safe along the turbulent waters of the Wild Atlantic Way.

Visitors can climb to the top of the lighthouse and enjoy the stunning views of the coastline, the Atlantic Ocean, Lough Swilly, and North Donegal. The tour will teach you all about the former lighthouse keepers and give you a more in-depth history of the lighthouse. A virtual reality experience will take you through the storm and sea that shipwrecked the Saldhana.

Ticket prices reflected below will give you a guided tour of the lighthouse and admission to the grounds and exhibition spaces. You must be at the lighthouse at the time you have selected for your tour. Please note that children must be a minimum of four feet to climb the lighthouse.

Ticket type	Price
Adult	€ 10
Child (five and up)	€ 5
Child (under five)	Free
Family (two adults and up to three children)	€ 33
One adult family	€ 18

Keem Bay

Address: Keem Beach, County Mayo

Keem Bay will give you many activities to enjoy, especially if you are an outdoor or kayak enthusiast! If you hike the trail along the Cliffs of Benmore, this is where you will be rewarded with some of the most beautiful views of the bay.

As for kayaking, there are kayak tours available during the summer. If you're experienced, you'll get to go past the Keem Strand and explore the stunning blue waters by the Croaghaun Sea Cliffs. Otherwise, novice kayakers can try and adventure around the quaint and tranquil Keel Lake.

Just outside of Keem Bay, wander through the abandoned village of Bunowa. No one knows why the town is empty now, but it used to be a place where people once grazed cattle.

Inis Meáin

Inis Meáin is a tiny village in the Aran Islands, home to about 200 people. Visiting this small village will give you a peaceful and authentic Irish experience as it is one of the least visited islands.

This island has plenty of scenic routes to explore, especially by bicycle, giving you spectacular panoramic views—you can even see the Cliffs of Moher! Additionally, Inis Meáin has plenty of historical learning opportunities to explore, including the Dún Fearbhaí, a stone ring fort near the pier. For literature enthusiasts, a visit to the John Millington Synge is also a must, as this was once the home to the famous Irish playwright and poet who fell in love with this tiny village.

International Dark Sky Reserve

Address: Cools, Ballinskelligs, County Kerry, V23 KX74

Stargazing is always a fun pastime, but imagine doing this while you hear the ocean rolling in. Its mission is to preserve the natural darkness of the night sky by limiting light pollution, which has adverse effects on wildlife and our health. This excursion is perfect for stargazing enthusiasts as it allows for clear views of the stars and other astrological phenomena (when the sky isn't cloudy and the moon is out).

The International Dark Sky Reserve in County Kerry is the only one to become a gold-tiered reserve in the Northern Hemisphere. It's also the only reserve with a church, pub, graveyard, beaches, playground, and a chocolate factory. Coming here at night gives you an authentic way of looking at the stars, the same way the Irish once used them as a way to guide them.

Must try food in Wild Atlantic Ways

Irish Brown Bread with Smoked Salmon: Ireland is famous for its hearty

brown bread, often made with a mix of whole wheat and white flour. Pair it with locally sourced smoked salmon, a specialty along the Atlantic coast. The combination of the nutty brown bread and the smoky, tender salmon creates a delicious and satisfying snack or light meal.

Dulse: Dulse is a type of edible seaweed that grows along the Atlantic coast of

Ireland. It's often harvested and dried to be enjoyed as a nutritious and salty snack. You can find dulse in various forms, such as dried leaves or flakes. Sampling this local delicacy provides a unique taste of the sea and a healthy alternative to traditional snacks.

Seafood Chowder: The Wild Atlantic Way is renowned for its fresh seafood. Seafood chowder, a hearty and creamy soup filled with a variety of fish, mussels, shrimp, and sometimes smoked salmon, is a must-try. Enjoy this comforting dish with a slice of crusty bread while overlooking the Atlantic Ocean for a true coastal experience.

Where to Stay Along the Wild Atlantic Way

Given that the Wild Atlantic Way is a long trek from the northern part of the Republic of Ireland to the southern part, if you plan to do this as one full trip, it's good to know some of the best places to stay! Of course, these are all recommendations and plenty of others will suit your budget on your trip to Ireland.

Staying in Donegal Town

Since Donegal Town is small, you don't need much time to check out the sites. You can easily do it in one day, then kick back for the evening! Here are some of the hotels to look into if you're going to make a stop in Donegal Town:

The Abbey Hotel: The Abbey Hotel is a mid-budget stay in Donegal Town overlooking the Donegal Bay and River Eske and putting you within walking distance of several pubs!

The Gateway Lodge: The Gateway Lodge is perfect if you only stay in Donegal Town for the night. This accommodation is close to Donegal Castle and 26 miles from Enniskillen!

Staying in Westport

Plenty of things to do in Westport will make staying in the town worthwhile, even for two days! Here are a couple of options to check out:

Knockranny House: This hotel has unique views overlooking the Croagh Patrick and Clew Bay islands. It's undoubtedly luxurious with its spacious rooms. In addition, you can enjoy a full Irish breakfast every morning.

Boffin Lodge Guest House: Situated in the historical quay area of Westport, the Boffin Lodge Guest House has beautifully furnished rooms and is within a short distance of several beaches along the Wild Atlantic Way. This bed and breakfast also offers a full Irish breakfast with pancakes, muffins, eggs, and salmon.

Staying in Clifden

Clifden's lively atmosphere will make for a beautiful place to spend a night or two! There is plenty of accommodation within the area. Here are a couple of options to check out:

Sea Mist House: The Sea Mist House is a beautiful bed and breakfast located in the heart of town. This accommodation offers a delicious breakfast and a small fridge to cool some snacks or water. It's also within walking distance of the supermarket. This budget-friendly bed and breakfast ranges from about €40 to 55 per person per night.

Mallmore County House: Set in a historic home dating back to the 1700s, the Mallmore County House is an excellent accommodation if you don't want to be in the heart of Clifden. The house is about a mile outside of Clifden (just south of the harbor) and offers an award-winning breakfast and beautiful gardens to enjoy in the summer months.

Staying in Dingle or Killarney

County Kerry has plenty to explore over a few days. Check out these accommodations as you travel through the area and make your way down (or up) the Wild Atlantic Way:

Pax Guest House: The Pax Guest House is one of the most unique accommodations in Dingle. This hotel has plenty of room options on the ground floor. It's so bright and offers you some of the best views of the water. The hotel is about mid-to-high range based on when you're going. But it's worth it if you're in Dingle for a few days!

Killarney Dromhall Hotel: The beautiful Killarney Dromhall Hotel is a family-owned accommodation with beautiful rooms and an outdoor terrace. It's situated near several cycle paths and the Muckross House.

What NOT to Do Along the Wild Atlantic Way

When following the Wild Atlantic Way, there are some things you should avoid doing to ensure you have a safe and enjoyable trip.

Don't Ignore Safety Precautions on Cliffs

The cliffs along the Atlantic Way routes are stunning but can be dangerous. Avoid getting too close to the edges, especially in windy conditions, and adhere to safety guidelines.

Don't Drive the Ring of Kerry

The Ring of Kerry is a famous drive in Ireland, but it doesn't offer much scenery, is overcrowded with tour buses, and is very narrow to drive quickly. Plus, you must pay to see some of their attractions, including the Kerry Cliffs.

Avoid this area altogether and drive the Dingle Peninsula instead. You'll be rewarded with fantastic views, filming locations from the Star Wars films, and charming small towns.

Don't Forget to Follow the Road Signs on Slea Head Drive

Although using your GPS or phone to help you navigate along Slea Head Drive, remember to follow the signs along the way. The signs posted help to keep the flow of traffic moving swiftly.

Don't Rush Past Cyclists and Walkers on Slea Head Drive

Cyclists and walkers also use Slea Head Drive. Be sure that if you come across them, give them plenty of space and drive past them safely. In addition, farmers with sheep and cows also use the roads, so be prepared to slow down and stop as they help guide the animals across.

Don't Ignore Local Artisan Products

Explore local markets and artisan shops along the route. Avoid missing out on unique handmade crafts, local cheeses, and other artisanal products.

The Wild Atlantic Way is a wild adventure along Ireland's west coast, with plenty of things to see, do, and explore. This is one of the most beautiful and scenic routes, with history and picturesque towns, leaving you with a genuine appreciation of the island.

Now that we have explored the Wild Atlantic Way let's move to the east side of Ireland and learn more about its historical essence and atmosphere and the things to do and not do while there.

Chapter 8:

The East Ireland—Dos and Don'ts

T he east side of Ireland is well-known and loved for its historic essence and atmosphere. After all, it is called Ireland's "Ancient East." On this part of the island, you can explore some of Ireland's most extraordinary outdoor adventures, archaeological sites, and beautiful homes from the eighteenth century. Uncover what makes Ireland's Ancient East so captivating when you visit and experience several of these attractions!

What to DO in the East of Ireland

The east of Ireland is expansive, with plenty of villages and towns to explore. We'll explore the various things to do in many different towns! Get out your map and mark down some things you'd love to see and do if you're on the east side!

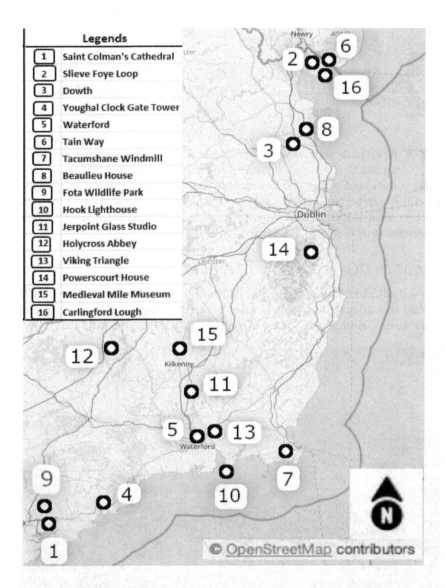

Legends	
1	Saint Colman's Cathedral
2	Slieve Foye Loop
3	Dowth
4	Youghal Clock Gate Tower
5	Waterford
6	Tain Way
7	Tacumshane Windmill
8	Beaulieu House
9	Fota Wildlife Park
10	Hook Lighthouse
11	Jerpoint Glass Studio
12	Holycross Abbey
13	Viking Triangle
14	Powerscourt House
15	Medieval Mile Museum
16	Carlingford Lough

© OpenStreetMap contributors

Saint Colman's Cathedral

Address: 5 Cathedral Pl, Kilgarvan, Cobh, County Cork

We will return to Cobh in County Cork to explore Saint Colman's Cathedral, the stunning church overlooking Cork Harbor's skyline. Up close, this cathedral's architecture is one to marvel at, especially its 100-meter high spire and the 49-bell carillon within the tower ringing its beautiful sounds. It's a tranquil atmosphere if you want to step away from the hustle and bustle of Cork for a little while.

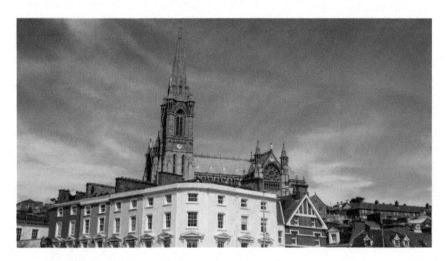

Tours are available, but you must make arrangements ahead of time. Their email is info@cobhcathedrapparish.ie.

Slieve Foye Loop

Address: Tourist Information Office, Carlingford, County Louth

The Slieve Foye Loop offers a challenging trek around a 5.5-mile loop. Don't worry—although it can be a challenging hike, you'll be rewarded with beautiful scenery throughout! The hike will take around 2.5 hours (depending on your fitness level or if you stop to take a breather). You will find yourself walking along roads, forest-covered roads, grassy tracks, and paths along the mountain, which can sometimes be wet and boggy. It sounds treacherous, but it's worth it for the beautiful mountain views and vistas overlooking the Carlingford Lough. You'll return to Carlingford at the end of your hike. Be sure to pop into one of their pubs or cafés for refreshments and a pint or tea to finish your day.

Dowth

Address: Glebe, County Meath

The archaeological site of Dowth is one of UNESCO's World Heritage Sites, Brú na Bóinne. This remarkable area is about 5,000 years old and is known for its well-preserved carvings and inscriptions on the large kerbstones. The tomb is unique, with two passage tombs on the western side. However, there isn't any access to explore the tombs for safety reasons. Nonetheless, this is a remarkable site for free and will make for great photos!

Youghal Clock Gate Tower

Address: 89 N Main St, Youghal-Lands, Youghal, County Cork, P36 EH56

Youghal Clock Gate Tower has plenty of history, tragedy, rebellion, love, and friendship within its walls, dating back 700 years. At this attraction, you'll be fully immersed with an active tour leading you through the past of the tower, from the bustling trading life of the medieval times, the years when the clock tower served as a jail, the battle of freedom in 1798, and the years of the wars. This converted tower will bring you through exciting exhibitions, Youghal's history, and see how the clock tower works. You will also get to see panoramic views of the town!

This attraction closes during the off-peak season. If you're curious about taking a tour, check the website in the spring or contact them at tours@livingyoughal.ie.

Celtic Ways Ireland

Take a fully organized tour of Ireland with the Celtic Ways Ireland tour company, bringing you on fantastic excursions that will take you away from the main attractions. These unique adventures will have you seeing plenty of hidden gems in Ireland, taking you along various landscapes from the mountains to hiking to kayaking and much more! All of these tours are tailor-made to suit your adventure needs. This is a fantastic way to explore Ireland with an expert guide. All tours include guides, accommodations, transportation, and packed lunches and dinners.

You can book your tour with Phil and Elaine at info@celticwaysireland.com.

Christ Church Cathedral

Address: Cathedral Square, Waterford, County Waterford X91 A447

Hours of operation:

Between April and October, the cathedral is open for tours from 10 a.m. to 5 p.m. Mondays to Saturdays. However, there will be some Mondays, Thursdays, and Fridays when the church will close at 4 p.m. to accommodate staff leave.

Between November and March, the cathedral is open for tours from 12 p.m. to 2 p.m. Mondays to Saturdays.

Standing in the heart of the Viking Triangle in Waterford is the Christ Church Cathedral, dating back to the eleventh century. This was where the English knight Strongbow and Princess Aoife were married in 1170. This church became more significant in the late thirteenth century when the Normans took over Waterford and built a new Gothic-style church, a focal point in the city until this church was built in 1773. Due to the cathedral's location, you will see several noteworthy features, including a pillar from the former medieval church.

It is free to visit the cathedrals during services. However, if you want to see the church on any other occasion, it's best to purchase a "Freedom of Waterford-Value Pass," allowing you to visit five attractions within the Viking Triangle. This pass is €15 per person. Children under 12 are free with an adult.

Táin Way

Looking for a two-day hiking excursion? The Táin Way is one of East Ireland's best-kept secrets in Louth. This long hiking trail spans almost 26 miles in a loop, bringing you to some of the highest peaks, landscapes steeped with legends, and scenery that will make you wonder what life was like all those years before.

Some legends and myths believe this route was once followed by Cú Chulainn, the legendary Irish hero, following his battle against the army of Queen Maeve of Connacht.

You can access the hiking loop in three towns: Carlingford, Omeath, and Ravensdale. Following the trail, you can explore ancient sites, such as King John's Castle from the twelfth century and Clermont Cairn, a neolithic burial cairn.

What to Enjoy in the East of Ireland

With the East of Ireland being an outdoor enthusiast's perfect playground, there are many things to see and do. Let's look at other things you should enjoy while exploring this side of the island!

Tacumshane Windmill

Address: Tucumshane, Broadway, County Wexford

The Tacumshane Windmill is the last surviving windmill in all of Ireland. It was built by Nicolas Moran in 1846 with timber from shipwrecks; this windmill was an alternative to a watermill for grinding grain to make flour for the local community. The uniqueness of the windmill is its thatched cap that helps the sails catch their wind.

This unique monument in Ireland is free to visit. You can obtain the key from the nearby Millhouse Bar & Restaurant.

Beaulieu House and Gardens

Address: Cross, Beaulieu, Drogheda, County Louth, A92 PD3R

Hours of operation: By appointment only. Guided tours can be accommodated for groups of 10 to 25 people. You can make further inquiries by emailing beaulieu.house.garden@gmail.com.

The Beaulieu House and Gardens is a beautiful seventeenth-century home with stunning gardens carefully manicured and restored to their former glory. The house is a prime example of authentic Irish architecture and was once the home to two separate families: the Plunketts and the Tichbournes.

As you tour the house, admire the beautiful interior fittings, the wood carvings with intricate designs, and the paintings from renowned Irish artists. The gardens are also a perfect way to take a lovely stroll, especially for plant lovers!

Hook Lighthouse

Address: Churchtown, Hook Head, County Wexford

Hours of operation: 9:30 a.m. to 5 p.m. daily

Explore one of Ireland's oldest standing and operational lighthouses in the world, Hook Lighthouse, built over 800 years ago by Knight William Marshal. The tower stands about 35 meters high and has been an essential guide for ships sailing through the treacherous waters of the St. George's Channel.

At this lighthouse, you will be guided up the 115 well-worn steps, spiraling up to the top to explore the chamber. You will get a chance to learn about the real-life stories of several of the light keepers and their families when you reach the balcony. Enjoy panoramic coastline views and see the graveyard where over 1,000 ships perished, including the seventeenth-century Great Lewis boat.

For more added fun, the Hook Lighthouse plays host to several festivals throughout the year, including the Maritime Matters and Pirate Festivals. There are so many things to enjoy and do here, so be sure to check what is happening when you're planning to go!

Ticket type	Price
Adult	€ 12
Child (5 to 17 years old)	€ 6
Student (with ID)/senior	€ 10
Assisted visitors (two tickets with proof of carer)	€ 10
Family of two (one adult and one child)	€ 16
Family with two children (one adult and two children)	€ 20
Family of three (two adults and one child)	€ 26
Family of four (two adults and two children)	€ 30
Family of five (two adults and three children)	€ 34

Jerpoint Glass Studio

Address: Jerpoint Glass, Glenmore, Stoneyford, County Kilkenny, R95 WN67

If you have never seen a glass piece being shaped into something beautiful, you must go to the Jerpoint Glass Studio in Glenmore. This family-run business has been around since 1979 and is skilled at glassblowing and turning molten glass into beautiful designs.

In the studio, you will see the glassmakers at work as they make their pieces by hand and watch a glassblowing demonstration. It's a magical experience watching the glassblowers turn the red-hot molten glass into various shapes and sizes! It's an exciting experience, especially seeing how the process starts and finishes!

Holycross Abbey

Address: Holycross Abbey, Holycross, Thurles, County Tipperary

Holycross Abbey is a Cistercian abbey well worth exploring, dating back to 1168. The tours of this abbey will take you back in time to how Holycross got its name and its essential role in various political and religious landscapes. You'll also explore Ireland's oldest church bell, Michael.

While here, it's worth it to wander around the Padre Pio meditation garden, look at the True Cross, and see the last remaining medieval chapter house doorway.

For more exploring in the area, wander through the Holycross village, where you will see plenty of cottages with thatched roofs. This place is so sacred in Ireland, and being able to enjoy it will give you a better understanding of Ireland's overall history.

Guided tours are the only way to see Holycross Abbey, which runs every Sunday between March and September at 2:30 p.m. The abbey asks that you book your tour at least 48 hours in advance. You can email them at holycrossabbeytours@gmail.com.

Epic Tours of the Viking Triangle

Address: Bishop's Palace, Viking Triangle, County Waterford

Go back to the era of the Vikings on a tour of the Viking Triangle. On this tour, you will learn about six important monuments that date back between 1190 and 1783 and the significance of Vikings in Waterford's history.

Your guide will take you through the Christ Church Cathedral, the Bishop's Palace, Reginald's Tower, Choristers' Hall, Greyfriars' Medieval Franciscan Friary, and the Mayor's Wine Vault. This tour lasts about 45 minutes and is run daily at 12 p.m., 2 p.m., and 4 p.m.

Ticket type	Price
General Admission	€ 10
Child	Free

Powerscourt House and Gardens

Address: Powerscourt Demesne, Enniskerry, County Wicklow
Hours of operation: 9:30 a.m. to 5 p.m. daily

Once the home to Lord Powerscourt and his family for over 400 years, this magnificent house is one to enjoy and explore through its beautiful rooms and expansive gardens tucked along the Wicklow Mountains.

The house is rich with history within its eighteenth-century walls—though its history goes back even further to when it was once a thirteenth-century castle before it was transformed into the majestic Palladian mansion you see today. The house has also been used for various films and movies, including BBC's The Tudors and the Excalibur.

At the house, you'll find plenty of shops and the Avoca Terrace café to enjoy a leisurely break. However, you will want to explore the gardens for an hour or two! These beautifully manicured Japanese and Italian gardens are worth exploring with their exotic plants and vibrant colors.

Ticket type	Address
Adult	€ 9
Child (6 to 16 years old)	€ 4
Child (under five)	Free
Senior (65 and up)	€ 8
Student (with valid ID)	€ 7.50
Family (two adults and three children)	€ 20

Medieval Mile Museum

Address: Gardens, Kilkenny City, County Kilkenny R95 K276

Hours of operation:

Between March and October: 9:30 a.m. to 4:30 p.m. daily

Between Thursdays to Mondays: 9:30 a.m. to 4:30 p.m. from November to February

During these months, the museum is closed on Tuesdays and Wednesdays.

Be prepared to return to the thirteenth century when you visit the Medieval Mile Museum in County Kilkenny. This museum is housed in a converted church that was once the site of St. Mary's cruciform and graveyard and will take you through 800 years of the country's history.

A main highlight to look for while at the museum is exploring the Kilkenny room, which contains several rare artifacts and treasures from Kilkenny's medieval times, as well as some replicas of the Ossary High Crosses. Other must-see areas in this museum include the Rothe Chapel, which has the tombs of the former Rothe family.

Self-guided tours are an option. However, if you want a more in-depth experience, guided tours will take you through the museum and the graveyard.

Self-Guided Tours

Ticket type	Price
Adult	€ 9
Students/seniors	€ 7.50
Children (under 16)	€ 4.50
Family (two adults and up to four children under 16)	€ 20

Museum and Graveyard Guided Tour

Please note the guided tour times depending on the months you will be in Ireland.

Between March and October: Museum guided tour: 10 a.m. and 2 p.m. daily. Graveyard tour: 3 p.m. daily

Between November and February:

Monday, Thursday, and Friday: Museum guided tour: 10 a.m., 11 a.m. and 2 p.m., Graveyard tour: 3 p.m.

Saturday and Sunday: Museum guided tour: 10 a.m. and 2 p.m., Graveyard tour: 3 p.m.

Ticket type	Price
Adult	€ 12
Student/Senior	€ 9.60
Child (under 16)	€ 6
Family (two adults and up to four children under 16)	€ 30

Carlingford Greenway Bike Hire

Address: Newry St, Liberties of Carlingford, Carlingford, County Louth, A91 FP9F

Hours of operation: 10 a.m. to 5 p.m., Monday to Friday

10 a.m. to 6 p.m., Saturdays

11 a.m. to 6 p.m., Sundays

If there is one great way to explore some of Ireland's towns, it's by hiring a bicycle for the day! The Carlingford Greenway Bike Hire is in the heart of Carlingford and offers bikes for hire in various forms, including electric and hybrid bikes, kids bikes, child seats, and bicycle trailers. The bikes will allow you to cover more of the town efficiently while exploring the area. The excellent staff at Carlingford Greenway can also help you with routes to work within the timeframe you'll have the bicycle for.

Adult and Teen Hybrid Bike and Add-Ons

Hire type	Price for three hours	Price for eight hours
Adult	€ 15	€ 25
Kids (between 6 and 11 years old)	€ 10	€ 15
Two-seater kids trailer (ages two to five)	€ 10	€ 10
Child seat (between 1 and 3 years old)	€ 5	€ 10

Electric Bike

The bike hire for electric bikes is only reserved for those who are 16 years old and up. The price is the same as rent, and they can be hired for four to eight hours.

Hire type	Price
Adult	€ 50
Children (1 to 4 years old)	€ 5
Two-seater kids trailer (2 to 8 years old)	€ 10

Carlingford Lough Ferry

Address: Greenore Port, The Harbour, Greenore, County Louth

Hours of operation: Monday to Friday: 10:30 a.m. to 6:30 p.m. and Saturdays and Sundays: 10:30 a.m. to 7:30 p.m.

Cross the Carlingford Lough by boat and explore the sites from the water! This ferry ride connects you from Green Greencastle in County Down to Greenore in County Louth, offering you some of the most scenic views of the Mourne Mountains and Cooley Peninsula! This ferry ride can be booked for your traveling pleasure but is also included with guided tours, including ones that will bring you up close and personal with the mountains! As you set sail, be sure to be on the lookout for wildlife. You may be lucky to see Finn the Dolphin, who regularly jumps and plays alongside the ferry!

Cars, camper vans, and motor homes can also go on this ferry if you are renting a vehicle for your travels.

Foot Passengers and Bicycles

Ticket type	Foot passenger (one way)	Foot passenger (return)	Bicycle (one way)	Bicycle (return)
Adult	€ 6	€ 9	€ 7	€ 10
Child	€ 5	€ 7	€ 5	€ 7
Family (two adults and two children)	€ 15	€ 20	€ 14	€ 22

Cars, Camper Vans, and Motor Homes
All prices reflected include the passengers per vehicle.

Ticket type	Price (one way)	Price (return)
Small cars or vans	€ 20	€ 30
Camper vans	€ 25	€ 35
Motor homes	€ 29	€ 40

Where to Stay in the East of Ireland

As this chapter is focused on the entire east side of Ireland, plenty of accommodations will be perfect, depending on which county you're in!

Barberstown Castle: Feel like royalty when you stay in the Barberstown Castle, a four-star hotel set in a thirteenth-century building. This hotel has a selection of suites to suit your traveling needs.

Glenview Hotel: Nestled in 30 acres of beautifully landscaped gardens and woodland walks, the four-star Glenview Hotel is set in County Wicklow, offering a tranquil way to relax after exploring the nearby towns. This hotel has plenty of rooms to suit your needs, including family suites.

The Foxrock Inn: The Foxrock Inn bed and breakfast is near the bottom of the Slieve Bloom Mountains. This accommodation is budget-friendly, ranging from €40 to €45 per adult, half of that if you travel with children between 2 and 12 years old.

Scholar's Townhouse: With over 150 years of history, the Scholar's Townhouse offers various room types to suit your traveling needs, including single and family rooms. The hotel is a bit on the higher range but puts you close to several attractions in Drogheda.

Bramble Rock: Bramble Rock is a family-run bed and breakfast in County Wicklow. The bed and breakfast rates are low to mid-range based on the room type, and breakfast is offered between 8 a.m. and 9 a.m. Please note that this bed and breakfast cannot accommodate children.

Tudor Lodge B&B: Tudor Lodge is a family-run bed and breakfast offering spacious rooms for travelers. Breakfast is provided every morning, and the accommodation is near several Slieve Bloom trails.

Otterstown House: The Otterstown House in Athboy, County Meath, is a family-run bed and breakfast offering rooms to suit any needs from single travelers to families. This little town is not too far from Dublin and other quaint towns and villages in the east part of Ireland, allowing you to explore more of the country!

Roundwood House: The Roundwood House is in County Laois, tucked into Slieve Bloom Mountains' lush parkland. Depending on your needs, this stunning accommodation offers bed and breakfast services and cottage rentals.

What NOT to do in the East of Ireland

Ireland's east side has plenty of things to do! But let's remember these tips to ensure your trip is safe and leaves the beauty untouched!

Don't Go Off the Trails on the Slieve Foye Loop

Remember to stay on the marked trails when hiking along the Slieve Foye Loop. Going off the trails can damage the local environment and wildlife. Not walking the Slieve Loop is advisable if the weather isn't great, as the terrain can become slippery and dangerous. This tip is also helpful if you follow the Táin Way. Stay on the well-marked paths, and don't divert!

The rich history, beautiful landscapes, and unique attractions in the east of Ireland will keep you going for several days! Whether you're interested in exploring the ancient archaeological sites, hiking the Slieve, or joining an adventure tour guide, you'll have plenty of things to consider if you stick to this side of the island! With all of Ireland's ancient secrets and history to discover, there is one more area to explore: Ireland's midlands.

Chapter 9:

The Midlands—Dos and Don'ts

The world is a book, and those who do not travel read only one page. –Saint Augustine

I reland's midlands tend to be the least visited area in the country. It may be because they are in the middle, and many travelers are more inclined to see the bigger cliff sites while experiencing the vibe in Dublin. But this area shouldn't be overlooked! Not only is the landscape beautiful for miles, but it's also rich with history and an excellent place for nature lovers to explore and escape from the hustle and bustle of the busier cities and towns. Let's explore what you should check out in the island's heart.

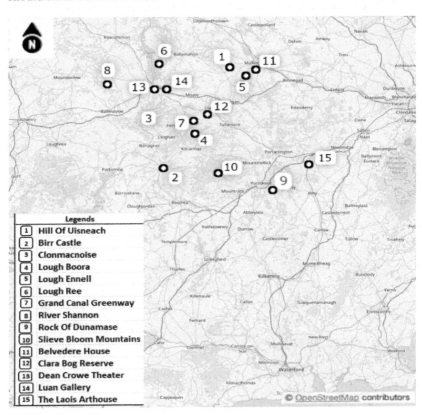

	Legends
1	Hill Of Uisneach
2	Birr Castle
3	Clonmacnoise
4	Lough Boora
5	Lough Ennell
6	Lough Ree
7	Grand Canal Greenway
8	River Shannon
9	Rock Of Dunamase
10	Slieve Bloom Mountains
11	Belvedere House
12	Clara Bog Reserve
13	Dean Crowe Theater
14	Luan Gallery
15	The Laois Arthouse

What to DO in the Midlands

Although Ireland's midlands don't have a coastline to explore the rolling ocean waves, this part of the country has many stones to uncover. Let's look at what to do while in the Midlands.

Hill of Uisneach

Address: Rathnew, Loughnavalley, County Westmeath, N91 R6C9

Hours of operation: 1) March to April: 1 p.m. on Saturdays and Sundays 2) May to September: 1 p.m. from Thursday to Sunday 3) October to February: 1 p.m. on Sundays

The Hill of Uisneach has a long history, dating back to the Neolithic and Bronze Ages. Although there isn't a definition for "uisneach" because it predates the Irish language, it has been dubbed a place where ceremonial sanctuaries took place, specifically the inauguration of the High Kings of Ireland.

There is plenty to learn at the Hill of Uisneach, including its mythology and archaeology stories. However, as this site is on a working farm and private land, you can only explore the Hill of Uisneach by a guided tour. The guided tour is a 1.8-mile walk, about two hours long, and must be pre-booked beforehand.

Ticket type	Price
Adult	€ 15
Students/seniors	€ 12
Children under 12	Free
Family (two adults and two children)	€ 25

Birr Castle

Address: Rosse Row, Birr, County Offaly, R42 VO27

Hours of operation: 9 a.m. to 4:30 p.m. daily

Birr Castle dates back to the Anglo-Norman Times. Its early occupants aren't known, but at some point, it was occupied by the O'Carroll family until the 1580s. Eventually, the castle became ruins, and it wasn't until Sir Laurence Parson's family took over the building that it was rebuilt and restored using some of the original parts, including the Central Gate Passage.

Birr Castle is rich in history, having survived two sieges and seen more changes throughout the years, including the construction of the Great Telescope in 1845.

This home is still a family home, so you won't be able to see everything. However, your general admission ticket will allow you to explore 120 acres of parkland, waterfall, Red Tree Trail, The Gallery Challenge, The Solar Trail, The Quest, The Engineering Trail, The Flora Trail (between April and June), 7-Gallery Science Center and Bird Spotter's Guide.

Ticket type	Price
Adult	€ 11
Child (under 17)	€ 6
Family (two adults and two children under 17)	€ 30

If you want to take a guided tour, this is available and will take you through five of the main rooms. Guided tours last an hour and run between May and September from Monday to Saturday at 10 a.m., 11:30 a.m., and 1 p.m. Guided tours are €20 per person, and it's recommended to prebook in advance.

Clonmacnoise

Address: Shannonbridge, Athlone, County Offaly, N37 V292

Hours of operation:

From November 1 to January 31: 10 a.m. to 5 p.m. (the last admission is at 4 p.m.). The car park barrier closes at 5 p.m.

From February 1 to March 12, 10 a.m. to 5:30 p.m. (the last admission is at 5 p.m.). The car park barrier closes at 5:30 p.m.

From March 13 to March 31: 10 a.m. to 6 p.m. (the last admission is at 5:30 p.m.). The car park barrier closes at 6 p.m.

From June 1 to August 31: 9 a.m. to 6:30 p.m. (the last admission is at 6 p.m.). The car park barrier closes at 6:30 p.m.

From September 1 to October 31: 10 a.m. to 6 p.m. (the last admission is at 5:30 p.m.). The car park barrier closes at 6 p.m.

Clonmacnoise is an ancient monastic site founded by St. Ciarán in the sixth century. This site became a central learning point for many scholars visiting from around Britain and Europe. Here, the scholars learned about religion and craftsmanship during the medieval times of Ireland.

Over the centuries, the monastery and its importance grew in size, with more scholars visiting from all over Europe. By the eleventh and twelfth centuries,

Clonmacnoise was a central production center of manuscripts with one of the most important and noteworthy books, Lebor Na hUidre, which translates to the Book of Dun Cow. It is one of the oldest manuscripts to survive and written entirely in Irish.

There is a museum and visitor center at Clonmacnoise that are worth exploring. Three high crosses are kept there to protect them from the weather, which you can see here (the replicas are outside). You can also learn more about the significance of this site in the museum and see other artifacts.

Ticket type	Price
Adult	€ 8
Senior	€ 6
Child/Student	€ 4
Family	€ 20

Lough Boora

Address: Boora, Leabeg, Tullamore, County Offaly

Hours of operation: Open all year round, 24 hours a day.

Lough Boora is a nature reserve that was once a cutaway peak bog in County Offaly and is a popular destination if you love spending time outdoors. There is a wide range of activities for any age to explore while at the reserve, including walking and cycling trails and a fairy trail, which is stroller and wheelchair accessible.

In addition to the nature reserve being an excellent place to wonder about, Lough Boora is a sanctuary for various species of wildlife. At the sculpture park, explore the 24 pieces of art that pay tribute to how we interact with nature, including the 60 Degrees Triangles and the Sky Train.

Lough Ennell

Lough Ennell is a large freshwater lake in County Westmeath, boasting scenic beauty, crystal-clear waters, and lush green shores to provide a fantastic backdrop for outdoor adventures. While at Lough Ennell, you can stroll around the lake's shoreline or hike through the nearby hills and forests to enjoy panoramic views of the surrounding landscape.

Lough Ennell is also an excellent spot to picnic if you want to enjoy a couple of hours. You'll also find that the Belvedere House and Gardens is also near the Lough Ennell.

If you're looking for places to camp in Ireland, camping is also available, and the grounds have excellent facilities.

Lough Ree

Lough Ree is the second largest lake along the River Shannon near the Clonmacnoise. This lake is popular for boating, water sports, and fishing. However, its claim to fame is its version of the Loch Ness Monster called the "Lough Ree Monster." Legends claim the creature resembles a sea serpent or giant eel, with its first sighting in the 1960s. Since then, many fishermen say they have seen this monster. But that's just a myth, and no scientific evidence supports that such a creature exists in the depths of the lake.

Monsters aside, the Lough Ree has plenty of areas to explore, including ancient settlements on the nearby islands of Inchcleraun and Saints Island. Several walking and cycling trails in the area, including the Lough Ree Heritage Trail, will lead you on a journey through the lake's history and ecology. It's also worth visiting the Barley Harbor on the eastern side of the lake if you want to check out a craft workshop. Not too far from the harbor is the town of Newtown Cashel, which also has plenty of sculptures to explore.

Grand Canal Greenway

The Grand Canal Greenway is a picturesque walking and cycling route running along the Grand Canal. Stretching across 82 miles, this route passes through several towns and villages, giving you stunning views of the Irish countryside (especially since much of the landscape has been untouched by today's modern society).

River Shannon

The River Shannon is the longest river in Ireland, stretching over 240 miles and through 17 counties.

The best way to explore and enjoy this river is on a boat! There are barge cruises that will take you along a journey where you will learn about the exciting ancient tales of kings and queens along with folklore creatures. You will also learn about the river's history and its strategic role in Ireland, including being a waterway for Vikings. Several castles, monastic settlements, and forts from various periods will also be seen. It's an exciting way to explore this long river while learning about the changes it saw throughout the centuries.

Rock of Dunamase

Address: Dunamaise, Aghnahily, County Laois

The Rock of Dunamase is a rocky outcrop with a fascinating history dating back to the ninth century, particularly with it being a significant defensive fortification through several battles and sieges. While it's primarily known for its Norman and medieval history, the Vikings also came to this site during their raids of Ireland.

Despite its ruinous state, the Rock of Dunamase remains popular in Ireland's midlands. You can take a hike to the top of the rock to take in the scenery from a higher altitude and explore the ruins of the castle, which give you a glimpse into its past. There are also ruins of a church and graveyard dating back to the tenth century.

Slieve Bloom Mountains

If you're keen on adventure, check out Slieve Bloom Mountain, where there are plenty of things to do. At the Slieve Bloom, you can rent a mountain bike and follow one of their many trails, which vary in difficulty. If mountain biking is not something you'd like to try, you can observe plenty of hiking and walking trails. Some of the top trails to explore on foot are the ones that will bring you through the Kinnitty Forest with your choice of three or six-mile trails to follow. However, the Kinnitty Loop is one of the most popular walking loops. The Kinnitty Castle is also a must-see!

Horseback riding is also an option. You can rent a horse from Birr Equestrian and tour the Slieve Bloom, which will take you through many valleys, the top of the mountains, and various boglands. These tours last about an hour.

Belvedere House and Gardens

Address: Mullingar, County Westmeath, N91 EF80

Hours of operation: 1) March and October: from 9:30 a.m. to 6 p.m. daily 2) April and September: from 9:30 a.m. to 7 p.m. daily 3) May to August: from 9:30 a.m. to 8 p.m. daily 4) November to February: from 9:30 a.m. to 4:30 p.m. daily

Special note: During the on-peak season, the house will close at 5 p.m., and during the off-peak season, it will close at 4 p.m.

Belvedere House and Gardens is a historic estate in County Westmeath. This impressive house was built for the first Earl of Belvedere, Richard Rochfort, in 1740 by renowned architect Richard Cassells. The home is as impressive on the outside as on the inside, but the tumultuous history of the Earl's life makes it more fascinating.

Rochfort was known to be an unkind and jealous man. He married Mary Molesworth when she was 16, settling in Robert's ancestral home, Gaulstown House. The couple had trialing years together, including rumors swirling that she committed adultery with Rochfort's brother, Arthur. Jealous and angry, Rochfort imprisoned Mary in the dungeons of Gaulstown House, where she remained until Rochfort died in 1774.

Explore the house's interior, where you will see how the building is the finest example of a Georgian home. Outside of the house is over 160 acres of parkland. Be sure to explore the several gardens, including the Belvedere Walled Garden and the Arboretum. The Jealous Wall is also worth exploring; it was built to block Rochfort's view of his other brother, George's, estate.

Ticket type	Price
Adult	€ 8
Student/Senior	€ 6
Child	€ 4
Family (two adults and two children)	€ 23

Clara Bog Nature Reserve

Address: Clara Bog Visitor Centre, Ballycumber Road, Clara, County Offaly, R35 T621

The Clara Bog Nature Reserve is one of Ireland's most interesting bogs, deep with a history that goes back thousands of years. It's believed that the bog was formed after the last Ice Age and has played a significant role in Ireland's landscape ever since.

For many years, the bog had many uses for communities, including harvesting purposes and providing fuel and energy. Unfortunately, bogs have disappeared in Ireland over the years, and given that this bog comprises 50% of the remaining uncut area, restoration efforts have been underway to preserve the Clara Bog Nature Reserve, keeping its thriving ecosystem alive.

The visitor center is worth the visit as it can teach you more about the conservation efforts and the biodiversity of raised bogs. You'll also learn about some archaeology and other interesting facts. In addition, taking a walk along the looped timber boardwalk is also a must-do while here.

What to Enjoy in the Midlands

Beyond adventuring and exploring the midlands, here are some things you can enjoy on your trip.

Dean Crowe Theatre

Address: 21 Chapel St, Athlone, County Westmeath

The Dean Crowe Theatre is a historic landmark theatre in the heart of Athlone. It's incredible to think that this building's life began as the St. Peter's parish and to see how far it has come since. More interesting is that the structure was built in two phases: the first phase in 1795 and the second sometime around 1809. The church served as a place of worship until the 1930s when the new church, SS Peter and Paul, became the new hall for St. Peter's parish.

By 1959, the building was renovated and got a new name: the Dean Crowe Theatre in memory of the beloved St. Peter's parish pastor, Dean John Crowe. Since its renovations, it has hosted many performances, including plays, musicals, concerts, and dance performances.

If you're interested in seeing what is playing, this is worth it for a night out!

Luan Gallery

Address: Elliot Rd, Athlone, County Westmeath
Hours of operation: Tuesday to Saturday: from 11 a.m. to 5 p.m., Sundays from 12 p.m. to 5 p.m., Closed on Mondays

The Luan Gallery is a must for art enthusiasts looking to admire some of the most exciting artists from Ireland's midlands. With floor-to-ceiling windows overlooking the River Shannon, explore the galleries and admire the various paintings, sculptures, photos, and art installations on display. The collections are changed every two months, so you'll never know what you will get to see when you go! This gallery is a free attraction.

The Laois Arthouse

Address: The Arthouse and Library, Stradbally, County Laois

The Laois Arthouse is one of the central points of creativity and culture. This arthouse has a year-round program for artists trying to develop their craft. Regular events, including art workshops, exhibitions, tours, and talks, are hosted throughout the year.

Dock Arts Center

Address: St. George's Terrace, Carrick-on-Shannon, County Leitrim, N41 T2X2
Hours of operation: 1) The building is open Mondays to Saturdays from 10 a.m. to 5 p.m. 2) The galleries are open Tuesdays to Saturdays from 10 a.m. to 5 p.m. 3) The Dock Arts Center is closed on bank holidays.

The Dock Arts Center is a multi-arts center devoted to theater, music, literature, and arts. There is something for everyone within its vibrant atmosphere. In addition, the Dock Arts Center has a lovely café where you can enjoy a small bite to eat when your event ends. Check out their website to see what events or exhibitions will happen when you visit Ireland!

Sean's Bar

Address: 13 Main Street, Athlone, Westmeath, W37 DW76
Hours of operation: Mondays to Thursdays from 10:30 a.m. to 11:30 p.m., Fridays and Saturdays from 10:30 a.m. to 12:30 a.m., Sundays from 12:30 p.m. to 11 p.m.

Sean's Bar is one of the oldest pubs in Ireland, welcoming visitors from around the globe. This pub dates back to the year 900 and earned its oldest pub recognition by the Guinness Book of World Records in 2004. Visit this pub and enjoy its atmosphere while sipping on a pint of Guinness or their branded whiskey.

Must try food in the Midlands

Lough Ree Pike: Lough Ree, one of the major lakes in the Midlands, is known

for its pike fish. Try freshly caught pike, prepared and cooked in various ways, such as pan-fried with butter and herbs. The delicate flavor of pike showcases the quality of the freshwater fish found in the region.

Lambs From Midlands: The Midlands are known for their excellent quality

lamb, thanks to the region's lush pastures. Taste dishes featuring tender Midlands lamb, such as roast lamb with rosemary and garlic or lamb stew with root vegetables. The natural sweetness and tenderness of the lamb are a treat for any meat enthusiast.

Barmbrack: Barmbrack is a traditional Irish fruitcake enjoyed during

Halloween. It's a sweet bread made with currants, sultanas, raisins, and sometimes candied peel. The dried fruits are soaked in tea before being added to the dough, infusing the cake with a rich, deep flavor. Sliced and spread with butter, barmbrack is a delightful tea-time treat.

Midlands Potato Dish: Potatoes are a staple in Irish cuisine, and the Midlands

region is no exception. Try a dish that showcases the versatility of potatoes, such as a hearty potato and leek soup, traditional colcannon (mashed potatoes mixed with cabbage or kale), or a delicious potato gratin. These dishes highlight the comforting and satisfying nature of Irish potatoes.

Where to Stay in the Midlands

Since Ireland's midlands will likely be your middle point on your journey, check out some of these accommodations to allow you a rest on your way and an opportunity to explore different areas you might have skipped over!

Glamping Under the Stars: Stay in style at the Glamping Under the Stars accommodation if you're looking to camp without the fuss. This accommodation suits all traveler types and offers small lodges, tents, and more.

Ardmore House: The quaint Ardmore House is a bed and breakfast in a period home with great views of the Slieve Bloom Mountains. This accommodation offers comfortable rooms, breakfast, and packed lunches if you require them.

Castle Durrow Country House Hotel: This accommodation is one of the midlands's hidden gems. Castle Durrow is in a mansion dating back to 1716. It's been fully restored and offers several different room options. Breakfast is also included with your stay.

Glasson Lakehouse: Located near the tranquil village of Glasson, the Glasson Lakehouse is a four-star hotel offering spacious rooms and takes you steps from several nearby attractions. There is also a golf course here if you want to play a round!

Kinnitty Castle Hotel: The Kinnitty Castle Hotel is located in the village of Kinnitty, with the Slieve Bloom Mountains set as the backdrop of this accommodation. Amazingly, this accommodation is rich with history dating back to the 1200s. This accommodation is a great option to stop on your journey, allowing you to explore the outdoors with a delicious breakfast.

Shamrock Lodge Hotel: The Shamrock Lodge Hotel is a mid-range accommodation in the heart of Athlone in County Westmeath. Plenty of free parking is available, and it is a five-minute walk from the town center.

Racket Hall Country House Hotel: The Racket Hall Country House Hotel is in the quaint heritage town of Roscrea. This accommodation is excellent if you travel with family as they offer family rooms. In addition, they have free parking and are just a short distance from Dublin and Limerick.

The Keadeen Hotel: The Keadeen Hotel was established in 1970 and is the longest-running accommodation in County Newbridge. This hotel is family-run and has beautiful gardens to relax in during the spring and summer months and a heated pool for your enjoyment. There is also breakfast available each morning.

What NOT to Do in the Midlands

With the Midlands containing some of Ireland's richest landscapes and ancient sites to explore, keep these in mind to ensure your trip is safe and monuments and bogs are preserved.

Don't Lean on the Monuments at Clonmacnoise

Given that the structures and monuments at Clonmacnoise are ancient, they are fragile. Be cautious as you explore the area and ensure you don't touch or lean on the stone crosses and monuments to ensure they remain preserved for the future.

Don't Swim in the River Shannon

The River Shannon is pretty, but you shouldn't go in it! Some of the rivers may have strong currents which can pull you under. Be mindful of safety regulations posted along the way to keep yourself and others safe.

Don't Expect to Fish Without a License at Lough Ennell

You will need a permit if you plan to try fishing at Lough Ennell. One-day licenses can be purchased online from Inland Fisheries Ireland.

Don't Disturb the Wildlife and Plants at the Bogs

Bogs are fragile ecosystems, and as you learned from the Clara Bog Nature Reserve, conservation efforts are being made to maintain them. Be mindful as you explore the Clara Bog Nature Reserve and other Ireland bogs to help the conservation efforts.

Ireland's Midlands might be an overlooked part of the country compared to the coastal areas, but they can offer unique perspectives of the country. There are plenty of things to explore and do in the middle of Ireland, including learning about the rich history while taking in the beautiful landscape.

Conclusion

I reland's rich history, ancient ruins, rolling hills, and cliffs will make for an unforgettable trip. Whether it's your first time in the country or your fifth, Ireland has much to explore and enjoy! As you go back through this book, remember the areas and attractions that resonated with you the most. There is a lot to choose from, and you won't be able to see everything on a single trip (unless you're spending several months in Ireland), so choose the ones you know are must-sees for this trip. This book has given you all the information you need to make informed choices for yourself and your journeys in the country! With Ireland close within your reach, explore the nation and its entirety to discover the true meaning of history in this historic European and United Kingdom island!

Glossary

All of the phrases and slang in this glossary have been provided by Matador Creators (2022).

Basic Irish Slang

- **Fierce**: This is a way to say "very." For example, "It's fierce cold outside."
- **He's/she's sound**: He's/she's cool.
- **I'm grand**: I'm good or alright.
- **I will in me arse**: I will not.
- **Jacks**: The restroom.
- **Jesus, Mary, and Joseph!** Oh my God or goodness!
- **Sickner for ya**: That is unfortunate for you.
- **What's the craic or story?**: How are you or what's new?

Northern Irish Slang Phrases and Words

- **Houl yer whisht**: A way to tell someone to be quiet.
- **I'll run ye over**: I'll give you a lift if you'd like.
- **I'm foundered**: A way to say, "I'm cold."
- **Quit yer gurning**: Stop complaining or moaning.

Other Quirky Irish Phrases

- **A tongin'**: To give someone a scolding.
- **Gobshite**: To call or refer to someone as an idiot.
- **He/she can talk the hinds off a donkey!** He/she is a chatterbox!
- **You could skin a cat out there!**: A way to express how cold it is outside.

Gaeilge Phrases

Most of Ireland speaks English, but you may find the odd Gaeilge spoken from time to time. These are some of the basic phrases you can use on your trip from 10 Basic Phrases in the Irish Language (Gaeilge) and Their Pronunciation (n.d.):

- **Cad is ainm duit?** (Pronounced cod is a-nim dit?): What's your name?
- **Conas atá tu?** (Pronounced kun-us a-taw too?): How are you?
- **Dia dhuit** (pronounced dee-ah gwit): Hello.
- **Go raibh maith agat** (pronounced guh rev mah ah-gut): Thank you.
- **Le do thoil** (pronounced luh duh hull): Please.
- **Slán agat** (pronounced slawn ah-gut): Bye (used when leaving a place).
- **Slán leat** (pronounced slawn lat): Bye (used when someone is leaving).
- **Tá mé go maith** (pronounced taw may guh mawh): I'm fine.

References

A guide to Inis Meáin (Inishmaan) Island. (n.d.). The Aran Islands. https://www.aranislands.ie/inis-meain-inishmaan-island

A new era at Slieve Donard. (n.d.). Slieve Donard. https://marineandlawn.com/slievedonard

About Hook Lighthouse. (n.d.). Hook Lighthouse & Heritage Centre. https://hookheritage.ie/about-us/about-hook-lighthouse

About Kylemore Abbey. (n.d.). Kylemore Abbey. https://www.kylemoreabbey.com/about

About Stormont Estate. (n.d.). Nidirect Government Services. https://www.nidirect.gov.uk/articles/about-stormont-estate

About the building. (n.d.). Northern Ireland Assembly. http://www.niassembly.gov.uk/assembly-business/office-of-the-speaker/80th-anniversary-open-day/about-the-building

About the Cliffs of Moher. (n.d.). Cliffs of Moher. https://www.cliffsofmoher.ie/about-the-cliffs-of-moher/?_ga=2.203159377.1579471910.1700522904-1115199195.1698690945

About us. (n.d.-a). Mizen Head Signal Station. https://www.mizenhead.net/aboutus.html

About us. (n.d.-b). Cranfield Alpacas. https://cranfieldalpacas.com/about-us

About us. (n.d.-c). Glasson Lakehouse. https://glassonlakehouse.ie/about-us

Accommodation at Castle Durrow. (n.d.). Castle Durrow Country House Hotel. Dublin

Adamson, A. (Director). (2005). The chronicles of Narnia: the lion, the witch and the wardrobe [Film]. Walt Disney Pictures.

Adamson, A. (Director). (2008). The chronicles of Narnia: Prince Caspian [Film]. Walt Disney Pictures.

Admission tickets. (n.d.). Christ Church Cathedral. https://christchurchcathedral.ie/admission-tickets

Amber. (n.d.). Is Cork, Ireland safe for travel in 2023? Crime & safety guide. Amber Everywhere. https://ambereverywhere.com/is-cork-ireland-safe

Amble In B&B. (n.d.). Discover Northern Ireland. https://discovernorthernireland.com/accommodation/amble-in-b-and-b-p694561

Apted, M. (Director). (2010). The chronicles of Narnia: The voyage of the Dawn Treader [Film]. Walt Disney Pictures.

Ardgillan Castle and Gardens. (n.d.). Visit Dublin. https://www.visitdublin.com/ardgillan-castle-and-gardens

Ardmore Country House bed and breakfast Kinnitty near Slieve Bloom Mountains. (n.d.). Ardmore Country House. https://kinnitty.com

Augustine, S. (2019). Saint Augustine quotes. BrainyQuote. https://www.brainyquote.com/quotes/saint_augustine_108132

Baird, E. (2023, June 26). A guide to visiting Elizabeth Fort in Cork. The Irish Road Trip. https://www.theirishroadtrip.com/elizabeth-fort

Bantry House and Garden. (n.d.). Bantry House & Garden. Retrieved November 14, 2023, from https://www.bantryhouse.com

Beara Way cycling route. (n.d.). Beara Tourism. https://bearatourism.com/things-to-do/beara-way-cycling-route

Beaulieu House and Gardens. (n.d.). Discover Ireland. https://www.discoverireland.ie/louth/beaulieu-house-and-gardens

Belfast Castle Estate & Cave Hill Visitor Centre. (n.d.). Visit Belfast. https://visitbelfast.com/partners/belfast-castle-estate-cave-hill-visitor-centre

Belfast Cathedral. (n.d.). Visit Belfast. https://visitbelfast.com/partners/belfast-cathedral-1

Belfast hop on hop off bus tour. (n.d.). City Tours Belfast. https://citytoursbelfast.com/belfast-hop-on-hop-off

Benioff, D. and Weiss, D. B. (Executive Producers). (2011–2019). Game of thrones. [TV Series]. HBO Entertainment; Television 360; Grok! Television; Generator Entertainment; Starling Television; Bighead Littlehead.

Birch, G. (2022, May 16). A guide to Lough Hyne: walks, night kayaking + things to do nearby. The Irish Road Trip. https://www.theirishroadtrip.com/lough-hyne

Birch, G. (2023a, January 18). A guide to visiting the Disney-like Belfast Castle (the views are incredible!). The Irish Road Trip. https://www.theirishroadtrip.com/belfast-castle

Birch, G. (2023b, June 3). Bed and breakfast Dublin: 11 brilliant b&bs in Dublin for 2023. The Irish Road Trip. https://www.theirishroadtrip.com/bed-and-breakfast-dublin

Birch, G. (2023c, June 3). Killarney hotels guide: 17 best hotels in Killarney (from luxury to pocket-friendly). The Irish Road Trip. https://www.theirishroadtrip.com/best-hotels-in-killarney

Birch, G. (2023d, June 4). 12 best things to do in Donegal Town (in 2023). The Irish Road Trip. https://www.theirishroadtrip.com/things-to-do-in-donegal-town

Birr Equestrian Centre. (n.d.). Discover Ireland. https://www.discoverireland.ie/offaly/birr-equestrian-centre

Book your greyhound racing admission. (n.d.). Curraheen Park. https://www.grireland.ie/go-greyhound-racing/our-stadiums/curraheen-park-greyhound-stadium/prices-deals/racing-admission

Booking. (n.d.). Water World Bundoran. https://www.waterworldbundoran.com/booking

Boorman, J. (Director). (1981). Excalibur. Warner Bros.

Botanic Gardens. (n.d.). Visit Belfast. https://visitbelfast.com/partners/botanic-gardens

Brown, V. (2016, November 25). A short history of Belfast City Hall. Culture Trip. https://theculturetrip.com/europe/united-kingdom/articles/a-short-history-of-belfast-city-hall

Bundoran Adventure Park. (n.d.). Www.discoverbundoran.com. https://discoverbundoran.com/locations/bundoran-adventure-park-2

Buy Belfast Zoo tickets. (n.d.). Belfast Zoo. https://online.belfastcity.gov.uk/zootickets/default.aspx

Buy tickets now! (n.d.). Carlingford Lough Ferry. https://tickets.carlingfordferry.com/?utm_source=carlingfordferry&utm_medium=internal

Callan, P. D. (2023, October 9). What not to do in Northern Ireland: 10 things you should never do. Ireland before You Die. https://www.irelandbeforeyoudie.com/what-not-to-do-in-northern-ireland-ten-things-you-should-never-do

Camila. (2023, March 31). 10 reasons why you should visit Ireland. Nordic Visitor. https://www.nordicvisitor.com/blog/10-reasons-visit-ireland

Carlingford Greenway bike hire. (n.d.). Discover Ireland. https://www.discoverireland.ie/louth/carlingford-greenway-bike-hire

Carlingford Lough Ferry. (n.d.). Discover Ireland. https://www.discoverireland.ie/louth/carlingford-lough-ferry

Carrick-a-Rede. (n.d.). National Trust. https://www.nationaltrust.org.uk/visit/northern-ireland/carrick-a-rede

Cassidy, A. (2023, October 5). These are Europe's friendliest cities—and Cork and Dublin rank very highly. Irish Examiner. https://www.irishexaminer.com/lifestyle/travel/arid-41239786.html

Castle Ward. (n.d.). National Trust. https://www.nationaltrust.org.uk/visit/northern-ireland/castle-ward

Castle Ward. (n.d.). Discover Northern Ireland. https://discovernorthernireland.com/things-to-do/castle-ward-p675331

Cave Hill Country Park. (n.d.). OutmoreNI. https://outmoreni.com/place/cave-hill-country-park

Cave Hill Country Park. (n.d.). Belfast City Council. https://www.belfastcity.gov.uk/cavehill

Celtic Ways Ireland. (n.d.). Our Celtic Ways. https://waterfordcamino.com

Chester Beatty. (n.d.). Visit Dublin. https://www.visitdublin.com/chester-beatty

Choose your experience. (n.d.). Guinness Storehouse. https://www.guinness-storehouse.com/en/booking?experience=SGI

Christ Church Cathedral. (n.d.). Visit Dublin. https://www.visitdublin.com/christ-church-cathedral

Christ Church Cathedral. (n.d.). Waterford. https://visitwaterford.com/vw_listing/christ-church-cathedral

Clara Bog Nature Reserve. (n.d.). National Parks & Wildlife Service. https://www.npws.ie/nature-reserves/offaly/clara-bog-nature-reserve

Clarke, G. (2023, October 21). 14 easy & accessible chair yoga poses to do at home or work. The Yoga Nomads. https://www.theyoganomads.com/chair-yoga-poses

Clifden Traditional Music Festival Clifden, Connemara, Co. Galway. (n.d.). Clifden Traditional Music Festival. http://www.clifdentradfest.ie

Clonmacnoise – history and significance. (n.d.). Enjoy-Irish-Culture.com. https://www.enjoy-irish-culture.com/Clonmacnoise.html

Clonmacnoise Monastery. (n.d.). Tuatha. https://www.tuatha.ie/clonmacnoise-monastery

Cobh. (n.d.). Pure Cork. https://www.purecork.ie/cobh

Colette. (2022, July 5). How to save money on a trip to Ireland. Ireland on a Budget. https://irelandonabudget.com/how-to-save-money-on-a-trip-to-ireland

Come explore nearly 1000 years of history. (n.d.). Christ Church Waterford. https://www.christchurchwaterford.com/tickets

Connemara National Park. (n.d.). National Parks of Ireland. https://www.nationalparks.ie/connemara

Corcoran, S. (2020, February 24). What is Dublin famous for? Premier Suites. https://www.premiersuiteseurope.com/en/blog/what-is-dublin-famous-for

Cork City Gaol. (n.d.). The Address Cork. https://www.theaddresscork.com/things-to-do/cork-city-gaol

Costa, V. (2022, December 21). Ireland named Europe's best travel destination - here's why so many Americans love it. Travel off Path. https://www.traveloffpath.com/ireland-named-europes-best-travel-destination-heres-why-so-many-americans-love-it

Cranfield Alpacas Experience - Kilkeel. (n.d.). Discover Northern Ireland. https://discovernorthernireland.com/things-to-do/cranfield-alpacas-experience-p751041

Crawford Art Gallery Cork. (n.d.). Crawford Art Gallery. https://crawfordartgallery.ie/about

Croke Park Stadium. (n.d.). Visit Dublin. https://www.visitdublin.com/croke-park-stadium

Croke Park Stadium tour. (n.d.). Croke Park. https://crokepark.ie/stadiumtour

Curtis, R. (Director). (2003). Love actually [Film]. Universal Pictures.

Cycling in Ireland. (n.d.). Ireland. https://www.ireland.com/en-ca/things-to-do/themes/cycling/cycling/?ds_c=TI_CA_EN_PRO_PM_All+Island_NA_IOI_NA_NA_NA_ACP_Ireland&ds_ag=Ireland%7CCycling&ds_k=biking+ireland&gad_source=1&gclid=CjoKCQjw-pyqBhDmARIsAKd9XIMWffmNs7NtWkwP7ASZxGwfkO-2cofe-HvZOPMb4HRwrMh7cqNsVSQaAmI_EALw_wcB&gclsrc=aw.ds

Daly, P. (2022, February 13). St. Valentine, hear my prayer: Why people flock to an unusual shrine in Dublin. CBC. https://www.cbc.ca/news/canada/newfoundland-labrador/valentines-day-shrine-irish-church-1.6345093

Deay, N. (2023, January 18). A guide to exploring Belvoir Forest Park in Belfast. The Irish Road Trip. https://www.theirishroadtrip.com/belvoir-park-forest/#Are_there_many_walks_in_Belvoir_Park

Delve into the deep. (n.d.). Marble Arch Caves. https://marblearchcaves.co.uk/tour_type/delve-into-the-deep

Derry. (2023, May 16). Exchanging dollars for euro for your trip to Ireland. Vagabond Tours of Ireland. https://vagabondtoursofireland.com/exchanging-dollars-for-euro-trip-to-ireland

Derry-Londonderry. (n.d.). Discover Northern Ireland. https://discovernorthernireland.com/destinations/derry-londonderry

Divis & the Black Mountain. (n.d.). Belfast Hills Partnership. https://belfasthills.org/visiting/divis

Donegal. (n.d.). Discover Ireland. https://www.discoverireland.ie/donegal/things-to-do

Donkin, A. E. (2023a, June 3). The best pubs, food + things to see in the Belfast Cathedral Quarter. The Irish Road Trip. https://www.theirishroadtrip.com/cathedral-quarter-belfast

Donkin, E. (2023b, January 18). A guide to visiting the historic Grand Opera House Belfast. The Irish Road Trip. https://www.theirishroadtrip.com/grand-opera-house-belfast

Donkin, E. (2023c, February). Bed and breakfast Westport: 11 brilliant b&bs in Westport for 2023. The Irish Road Trip. https://www.theirishroadtrip.com/bed-and-breakfast-westport

Donkin, E. (2023d, February 3). Westport hotels guide: 11 best hotels in Westport for a weekend away. The Irish Road Trip. https://www.theirishroadtrip.com/best-hotels-in-westport

Donkin, E. (2023e, June 26). A guide to visiting Garnish Island in Cork (the ferry, what to see + more). The Irish Road Trip. https://www.theirishroadtrip.com/garnish-island

Doolin Cave and visitor centre. (n.d.). Doolin Tourism. https://doolin.ie/doolin-cave-and-visitor-centre

Doolin Cave tour – book now. (n.d.). Doolin Cave. https://doolincave.ie/doolin-cave-tour/#

Dowth. (n.d.). Discover Ireland. https://www.discoverireland.ie/meath/dowth

Dowth Megalithic Passage Tomb. (n.d.). Newgrange.com. https://www.newgrange.com/dowth.htm

Dublin Castle. (n.d.). TimeOut. https://www.timeout.com/dublin/attractions/dublin-castle

Dublin Castle. (n.d.). Heritage Ireland. https://heritageireland.ie/places-to-visit/dublin-castle

Dublin tours & experiences. (n.d.). Jameson Distillery Dublin. https://www.jamesonwhiskey.com/en-ie/visit-our-distilleries/jameson-bow-street-distillery-tour

Dublin trams (Luas). (n.d.). Dublin. https://www.dublinpublictransport.ie/dublin-trams

Dunmore Head. (n.d.). Discover Ireland. https://www.discoverireland.ie/kerry/dunmore-head

East Ireland accommodation. (n.d.). Ireland Travel Guide. https://www.myirelandtour.com/travelguide/east-ireland/accommodation.php

East Ireland travel guide. (n.d.). Ireland Travel Guide. https://www.myirelandtour.com/travelguide/east-ireland/index.php

11 excellent things to do in Kildare. (n.d.). Discover Ireland. https://www.discoverireland.ie/kildare/things-to-do-kildare

Embark on a fantastic tasting experience at Walled City Brewery. (n.d.). Walled City Brewery. https://www.walledcitybrewery.com/experiences

EPIC The Irish Emigration Museum. (n.d.). Visit Dublin. https://www.visitdublin.com/epic-the-irish-emigration-museum

Epic tour of the Viking Triangle. (n.d.). Discover Ireland. https://www.discoverireland.ie/waterford/epic-tour-of-the-viking-triangle

Etiquette on transport. (n.d.). Transport for Ireland. https://www.transportforireland.ie/getting-around/etiquette-on-transport

Experience the most dramatic coastal walk in Europe. (n.d.). The Gobbins. https://www.thegobbinscliffpath.com

Explore 3 stunning walks in the Dublin Mountains. (n.d.). Visit Dublin. https://www.visitdublin.com/guides/dublin-mountain-walks

Explore Bushmills. (n.d.). Tripadvisor. https://www.tripadvisor.com/Tourism-g209948-Bushmills_County_Antrim_Northern_Ireland-Vacations.html

Explore Enniskillen. (n.d.). Fermanagh Lakelands. https://www.fermanaghlakelands.com/explore-enniskillen

Explore her history. (n.d.). Titanic Belfast. https://www.titanicbelfast.com/explore/ss-nomadic/explore-her-history

Fáilte go dtí An Cláchán Glencolmcille Folk Village. (n.d.). Glencolmcille Folk Village. https://www.glenfolkvillage.com/index.html

Fanad Lighthouse tours. (n.d.). Fanad Lighthouse. https://fanadlighthouse.com/tours

5 beautiful national parks of the Wild Atlantic Way. (2020, April 14). Vagabond Tours of Ireland. https://vagabondtoursofireland.com/most-beautiful-national-parks-wild-atlantic-way

5 tips for finding the perfect accommodation in Ireland! (2015, September 9). Go to Ireland.com. https://www.go-to-ireland.com/5-tips-for-finding-the-perfect-accommodation-in-ireland

Flying to Ireland. (n.d.). Discovering Ireland. https://www.discoveringireland.com/fly-to-ireland

Follow Me Away. (2022, November 23). Planning a trip to Ireland: 8 big mistakes to avoid. https://www.followmeaway.com/planning-a-trip-to-ireland

Friel, A. J. (2023, June 4). 11 beaches near Cork City (5 are under 40 minutes away). The Irish Road Trip. https://www.theirishroadtrip.com/beaches-near-cork-city

Galleries. (n.d.). Midlands Ireland. https://www.midlandsireland.ie/visit/galleries

Galway. (n.d.). Discover Ireland. https://www.discoverireland.ie/galway/things-to-do

Gaol experience and tours. (n.d.). Crumlin Road Gaol. https://www.crumlinroadgaol.com/tours-events

General admission ticket prices: (n.d.). Birr Castle. https://birrcastle.com/visitor-information

General Admissions. (n.d.). Blarney Castle & Gardens. https://ie.patronbase.com/_BlarneyCastle/Performances/List?prod_id=GA2&date=2023-11-21

Ghangas, S. (n.d.). 13 best things to do in summer in Ireland in 2023 for a chilled-out holiday. Travel Triangle. https://traveltriangle.com/blog/summer-in-ireland

Giant's Causeway. (n.d.). National Trust. https://www.nationaltrust.org.uk/visit/northern-ireland/giants-causeway

Giant's Causeway. (n.d.). Discover Northern Ireland. https://discovernorthernireland.com/things-to-do/giants-causeway-p742371

Glenveagh Castle: a historical treasure in County Donegal, Ireland. (n.d.). Irish History. https://irishhistory.com/architecture-and-monuments/castles/glenveagh-castle-a-historical-treasure-in-county-donegal-ireland

Gomez, T. (2023, July). 11 unmissable experiences on the Wild Atlantic Way in Donegal, Ireland. Brogan Abroad. https://broganabroad.com/wild-atlantic-way-donegal-ireland/#Meet_one_of_the_last_masters_of_Donegal_tweed

Grand Canal Greenway. (n.d.). Midlands Ireland. https://www.midlandsireland.ie/places/grand-canal-greenway

Guided Tours of Beaulieu House and Garden. (n.d.). Beaulieu House & Gardens. https://beaulieuhouse.ie/visitors

Guinness Storehouse. (n.d.). Visit Dublin. https://www.visitdublin.com/guinness-storehouse

Here are just some of the activities we recommend on your trip to the Gap of Dunloe.... (n.d.). The Gap of Dunloe. https://gapofdunloe.com/activities

Hill of Uisneach tours. (n.d.). Uisneach. https://uisneach.ie/tours

Hirst, M, Fellner, E., Bevan, T., Silverman, B. Weinberg, T., Hockin, S., & Waghmare, M. (Executive Producers). (2007–2010). The Tudors. [TV Series]. Reveille Eire; Working Title Television; Octagon Entertainment; Peace Arch Entertainment; Showtime Networks.

History. (n.d.). Belfast Castle. https://www.belfastcastle.co.uk/belfast-castle-about-us/history/history.aspx

History and heritage of Victoria Park. (n.d.). East Side Greenways. https://www.eastsidegreenways.com/history-and-heritage-of-victoria-park

History of the Hill of Uisneach. (n.d.). Uisneach. https://uisneach.ie/history

History of the site. (n.d.). Clara Bog Nature Reserve. https://www.clarabognaturereserve.ie/article-about/article-history-of-site

History.com Editors. (2023a, October 16). Who was St. Patrick. HISTORY; A&E Television Networks. https://www.history.com/topics/st-patricks-day/who-was-saint-patrick

History.com Editors. (2023a, October 18). Samhain. HISTORY; A&E Television Networks. https://www.history.com/topics/holidays/samhain

Holycross Abbey. (n.d.). Discover Ireland. https://www.discoverireland.ie/tipperary/holycross-abbey

Home page. (n.d.). Tudor Lodge B&B Tullamore. https://tudorlodgebandb.com

How to book things to do? | honest guide to booking tours & activities in ireland. (n.d.). Ollie's Tours. https://olliestours.com/blog/how-to-book-things-to-do-honest-guide-to-booking-tours-activities-in-ireland

How to contact emergency services in Ireland. (2021, April 22). Gov.ie. https://www.gov.ie/en/service/89da6-how-to-contact-emergency-services-in-ireland

Immerse yourself in world-class beauty. (n.d.). Powerscourt Estate, House & Gardens. https://powerscourt.com/?_gl=1

Ireland B&B adventure. (n.d.). Aer Lingus Vacation Store. https://www.aerlingusvacationstore.com/vacations/ireland-b-and-b-adventure?utm_source=colette&utm_medium=affiliate&utm_campaign=affiliate_US&utm_content=Content&ph_id=af

Ireland Before You Die. (2017, February 16). Top 10: facts about cork you didn't know.... https://www.irelandbeforeyoudie.com/top-10-facts-cork-didnt-know

Ireland tour companies. (n.d.). TourRadar. https://www.tourradar.com/g/ireland-tour-operators

Irish American Mom. (2019, July 14). 7 avoidable mistakes when planning a trip to Ireland. https://www.irishamericanmom.com/7-big-mistakes-to-avoid-when-planning-a-trip-to-ireland/#aioseo-5-staying-in-the-republic-of-ireland-only

Irish culture, manners, etiquette and politeness. (n.d.). Welcome to Limerick. https://welcometolimerick.weebly.com/irish-culture-manners.html

Irish sayings proverbs & blessings. (n.d.). Vagabond Tours of Ireland. Retrieved October 30, 2023, from https://vagabondtoursofireland.com/irish-sayings-proverbs-blessings

IrishCentral Staff. (2022, March 23). The beauty and danger of Blarney Castle's poison garden. IrishCentral. https://www.irishcentral.com/travel/poison-garden-blarney-castle

Iveagh Gardens. (n.d.). Visit Dublin. https://www.visitdublin.com/iveagh-gardens

Jack. (n.d.). The best places to exchange currency in Ireland. Spoketravel. https://spoketravel.com/the-best-places-to-exchange-currency-in-ireland

Jerpoint Glass Studio. (n.d.). Discover Ireland. https://www.discoverireland.ie/kilkenny/jerpoint-glass-studio

Karsten, M. (2023, April 5). Killarney National Park: Exploring mountains, lakes, and castles. Expert Vagabond. https://expertvagabond.com/killarney-ireland-travel-guide

Karsten, M. (2023, August 4). Everything you need to know before renting a car in Ireland. Expert Vagabond. https://expertvagabond.com/renting-car-in-ireland

Kay. (n.d.). 6 top things to do in Derry-Londonderry. The Chaotic Scot. https://www.thechaoticscot.com/things-to-do-derry-londonderry

Keem Strand. (n.d.). Ireland. https://www.ireland.com/en-ca/destinations/regions/keem-strand

Kerry International Dark-Sky Reserve. (n.d.). Discover Ireland. https://www.discoverireland.ie/kerry/kerry-international-dark-sky-reserve

Kilkenny City. (n.d.). Ireland. https://www.ireland.com/en-ca/destinations/county/kilkenny/kilkenny-city/?ds_c=TI_CA_EN_PRO_EM_Kilkenny_Kilkenny+City_IOI_NA_NA_NA_ACP_Location-Kilkenny&ds_ag=Kilkenny%7CGeneral&ds_k=what+to+do+in+kilkenny+ireland&gad_source=1&gclid=Cj0KCQjwy4KqBhDoARIsAEbCt6iFNjwKjwe5EOQKrZKwEv26GXB5OQHTWuh_CfeL8mrGWIItfa1UsVUaA078EALw_wcB&gclsrc=aw.ds

Kilmainham Gaol. (n.d.). Visit Dublin. https://www.visitdublin.com/kilmainham-gaol

Kinnitty Castle Hotel. (n.d.). Tripadvisor. https://www.tripadvisor.ie/Hotel_Review-g1515835-d276590-Reviews-Kinnitty_Castle_Hotel-Kinnitty_County_Offaly.html

Kylemore Abbey Tickets. (n.d.). Kylemore Abbey. https://kylemore.retailint-tickets.com/Home

Lamberg, E. (2023, July 21). Everything you need to know about travel insurance before you book your next trip. CNBC. https://www.cnbc.com/select/travel-insurance-guide

Lang, C. (2018, October 30). What is Samhain? What to know about the ancient pagan festival that came before Halloween. Time. https://time.com/5434659/halloween-pagan-origins-in-samhain

Leddin, G. (2023, October 9). What not to do in Ireland: 10 things you should never do. Ireland before You Die. https://www.irelandbeforeyoudie.com/what-not-to-do-in-ireland

Lennon, S. (2019, May 18). In pictures: conservation project starts at Kilteale Church. Laois Today. https://www.laoistoday.ie/2019/05/18/in-pictures-conservation-project-starts-at-kilteale-church

Location & opening hours. (n.d.). The Dock. https://www.thedock.ie/visit/location-opening-hours

Lough Boora. (n.d.). Midlands Ireland. https://www.midlandsireland.ie/places/loughboora-2

Lough Boora Discovery Park. (n.d.). Discover Ireland. https://www.discoverireland.ie/offaly/lough-boora-discovery-park

Lough Ennell. (n.d.). Midlands Ireland. https://www.midlandsireland.ie/places/lough-ennell

Lough Hyne. (n.d.). Pure Cork. https://www.purecork.ie/things-to-do/lough-hyne

Lough Hyne night kayaking tour. (n.d.). Atlantic Sea Kayaking. https://www.atlanticseakayaking.com/booking/lough-hyne-night-kayaking

Lough Ree. (n.d.). Midlands Ireland. https://www.midlandsireland.ie/places/lough-ree

Luan Gallery. (n.d.). Athlone. https://athlone.ie/things_to_do/luan-gallery

Lupascu, V. (2022, November 29). Where to stay in Cork, Ireland – the best neighborhoods with hotels for every budget. Miss Tourist. https://misstourist.com/where-to-stay-in-cork-ireland

Malahide Castle and Gardens. (n.d.). Visit Dublin. https://www.visitdublin.com/malahide-castle-and-gardens

Marble Arch Caves - Enniskillen. (n.d.). Discover Northern Ireland. https://discovernorthernireland.com/things-to-do/marble-arch-caves-p684491

March, J. (2023, January 19). A quick and easy guide to the very rewarding Ballycotton Cliff walk. The Irish Road Trip. https://www.theirishroadtrip.com/ballycotton-cliff-walk

March, J. (2023, January 19). Visiting the Baltimore Beacon: the walk, the history + nearby attractions. The Irish Road Trip. https://www.theirishroadtrip.com/baltimore-beacon

Marissa. (2023, August 9). 17 things not to do in Ireland as a tourist on your next trip - wander around IrelandIreland. Wander around Ireland. https://wanderaroundireland.com/things-not-to-do-in-ireland

Matador Creators. (2022, April 8). This guide to Irish slang and insults will have you downing Irelanduinness with the locals in a flash. Matador Network. https://matadornetwork.com/read/irish-slang

Mayo. (n.d.). Discover Ireland. https://www.discoverireland.ie/mayo/things-to-do

Mccourt, F. (1996). Angela's ashes. Flamingo.

McDonagh, M. (Director). (2022). The banshees of Inisherin [Film]. Searchlight Pictures.

McMurray, S. (2023, January 20). 14 top-rated things to do in winter in Ireland. Planet Ware. https://www.planetware.com/ireland/top-rated-things-to-do-in-winter-irl-1-35.htm

Meath. (n.d.). Discover Ireland. https://www.discoverireland.ie/meath/things-to-do

Medieval Mile Museum. (n.d.). Discover Ireland. https://www.discoverireland.ie/kilkenny/medieval-mile-museum

Merrion Square. (n.d.). Visit Dublin. https://www.visitdublin.com/merrion-square

Merrion Square Park. (n.d.). EGHN. https://www.eghn.org/en/merrion-square-park-2/#1452099273569-531e240e-68e2

Midland fisheries group permit. (n.d.). Inland Fisheries Ireland. https://permits.fishinginireland.info/product-category/midland-fisheries-group-permits/midland-fisheries-group-permit

Midleton Distillery Experience. (n.d.). Jameson Whiskey. https://www.jamesonwhiskey.com/en-ie/visit-our-distilleries/midleton-distillery-cork/?keyword=MIDPricingCalendar

Mizen Head. (n.d.). Mizen Head. https://mizenhead.ie

Mizen Head, County Cork. (n.d.). Ireland. https://www.ireland.com/en-us/destinations/county/cork/mizen-head

Monaghan. (n.d.). Discover Ireland. https://www.discoverireland.ie/monaghan

Mourne Trails & ales tour. (n.d.). Discover Northern Ireland. https://discovernorthernireland.com/things-to-do/mourne-trails-and-ales-tour-p751271

Mullen, E. (2023, February 17). 18 things you should never do in Dublin as a tourist. Lovin Dublin. https://lovindublin.com/dublin/18-things-you-should-never-do-in-dublin-as-a-tourist

Murchadh, O. Ó. (2022, May 13). A guide to visiting Glencolmcille Folk Village in Donegal. The Irish Road Trip. https://www.theirishroadtrip.com/glencolmcille-folk-village-donegal

Murchadh, O. Ó. (2023, January 19). 7 of the best hotels in Donegal town centre (and some swanky spots nearby). The Irish Road Trip. https://www.theirishroadtrip.com/best-hotels-in-donegal-town

Mussenden Temple. (n.d.). Atlas Obscura. https://www.atlasobscura.com/places/mussenden-temple

Nano Nagle Place. (n.d.). Cork City Council. https://www.corkcity.ie/en/cork-heritage-open-day/buildings/cultural-buildings/nano-nagle-place

National Museum of Ireland - natural history. (n.d.). Visit Dublin. https://www.visitdublin.com/national-museum-of-ireland-natural-history

Nesbitt, J. (n.d.). James Nesbitt quotes. BrainyQuote. https://www.brainyquote.com/quotes/james_nesbitt_686702?src=t_belfast

Nieman, L. (2018, August 30). The ultimate guide to the amazing town of Clifden Ireland. Wander Your Way. https://wanderyourway.com/the-ultimate-guide-to-the-amazing-town-of-clifden-ireland

Norah, J. (2023, July 9). Belfast travel guide: Top 40 things to do in Belfast Northern Ireland. Independent Travel Cats. https://independenttravelcats.com/top-things-to-do-in-belfast-northern-ireland

O'Brien, G. (n.d.). History of the Dean Crowe Theatre. The Dean Crowe Theatre. Retrieved November 28, 2023, from https://www.deancrowetheatre.com/history-of-the-dean-crowe-theatre/#1559750751280-dcfb2d70-9fa2057c-892b

O'Brien, G., & Castle, J. (2018). Nano Nagle—an unconventional woman. 18th-19th Century Social Perspectives, 26(4). https://www.historyireland.com/nano-nagle-an-unconventional-woman

O'Brien, M. (2014, August 29). Frank McCourt's words still echo on Limerick streets. The Sydney Morning Herald. https://www.smh.com.au/entertainment/frank-mccourts-words-still-echo-on-limerick-streets-20140826-1084de.html

O'Callaghan, G. (2021, January 15). Twelve famous films that have scenes shot in Cork. Cork Beo. https://www.corkbeo.ie/culture/twelve-famous-films-scenes-shot-19210362

O'Connell, R. (2020, August 1). Is Ireland safe? 6 tips from a traveler. World Nomads. https://www.worldnomads.com/travel-safety/northern-europe/ireland/how-to-stay-safe-while-traveling-ireland

O'Hara, K. (2023a, January 1). Irish culture: 9 things that make our little island tick. The Irish Road Trip. https://www.theirishroadtrip.com/irish-culture

O'Hara, K. (2023b, January 5). Pax House dingle: A luxury guesthouse with views that'll knock you sideways. The Irish Road Trip. https://www.theirishroadtrip.com/pax-house-dingle

O'Hara, K. (2023c, June 13). 28 best things to do in Cork in 2023. The Irish Road Trip. https://www.theirishroadtrip.com/what-to-do-in-cork

O'Hara, K. (2023d, July 28). 19 best things to do in Kinsale (food tours, forts, lively pubs and walks). The Irish Road Trip. https://www.theirishroadtrip.com/things-to-do-in-kinsale

O'Hara, K. (2023e, July 28). Where to stay in Dublin Ireland (the best areas and neighborhoods). The Irish Road Trip. https://www.theirishroadtrip.com/where-to-stay-in-dublin-ireland

O'Hara, K. (2023f, August 8). The best guide to renting a car in Ireland (2023). The Irish Road Trip. https://www.theirishroadtrip.com/renting-a-car-in-ireland

O'Hara, K. (2023g, September 8). What not to do in Ireland: 19 tips to remember. The Irish Road Trip. https://www.theirishroadtrip.com/what-not-to-do-in-ireland

O'Hara, K. (2023h, September 8). When is the best time to visit Ireland? A guide to weather, seasons + climate. The Irish Road Trip. https://www.theirishroadtrip.com/best-time-to-travel-to-ireland

O'Hara, K. (2023i, October 16). The key differences between Northern Ireland vs Ireland in 2023. The Irish Road Trip. https://www.theirishroadtrip.com/northern-ireland-vs-ireland

O'Hara, K. (2023j, November 3). Fun facts about Ireland: 36 weird, unusual and interesting Ireland facts. The Irish Road Trip. https://www.theirishroadtrip.com/facts-about-ireland

Offaly. (n.d.). Discover Ireland. https://www.discoverireland.ie/offaly/things-to-do

One pass, five experiences. (n.d.). Waterford Treasures. https://www.waterfordtreasures.com/open-museum

Opening hours. (n.d.). Titanic Belfast. https://www.titanicbelfast.com/visitor-information/opening-hours

Opening times. (n.d.). Ardgillan Castle and Gardens. https://ardgillancastle.ie/opening-times

Our packages. (n.d.). Bike Mourne. https://www.bikemourne.com/rostrevor-mountain-bike-hire

pcarroll. (n.d.). Facts about Limerick. Maldron Hotel. https://www.maldronhotellimerick.com/blog/10-interesting-facts-about-limerick

Phelan, K. (2019, September 25). 16 reasons why you should visit Ireland at least once in your lifetime. Culture Trip. https://theculturetrip.com/europe/ireland/articles/16-reasons-why-you-should-visit-ireland-at-least-once-in-your-lifetime

Phoenix Park. (n.d.). Visit Dublin. https://www.visitdublin.com/phoenix-park

Pietrzak, K. (2020, October 17). Where to stay in Cork: best areas and accommodations - your Irish adventure. Your Irish Adventure. https://youririshadventure.com/where-to-stay-in-cork

Plan a visit. (n.d.). Iveagh Gardens. https://iveaghgardens.ie/plan-a-visit

Poleon, J. (2022, July 10). Cape Clear Island: What to see, when to visit, and things to know. Ireland before You Die. https://www.irelandbeforeyoudie.com/cape-clear-island-what-to-see-when-to-visit-and-things-to-know

Portstewart Strand and Barmouth. (n.d.). Discover Northern Ireland. https://discovernorthernireland.com/things-to-do/portstewart-strand-and-barmouth-p675631

Powerscourt House & Gardens. (n.d.). Discover Ireland. https://www.discoverireland.ie/wicklow/powerscourt-house-gardens

Public transport. (n.d.). Ireland. https://www.ireland.com/en-us/help-and-advice/practical-information/public-transport

Racket Hall Country House Hotel. (n.d.). Tripadvisor. https://www.tripadvisor.ie/Hotel_Review-g1077202-d1088236-Reviews-Racket_Hall_Country_House_Hotel-Roscrea_County_Tipperary.html

Rainbolt, D. (2019, February 13). How St. Valentine found his way to Dublin. Wilderness Ireland. https://www.wildernessireland.com/blog/st-valentine-dublin

Revell, A. (2022, May 26). A guide to Inis Meáin Island (Inishmaan): things to do, the ferry, accommodation + more. The Irish Road Trip. https://www.theirishroadtrip.com/inis-meain-island

Revell, A. (2023, June 26). A guide to the mighty Priest's Leap in Cork. The Irish Road Trip. https://www.theirishroadtrip.com/priests-leap-drive

River Shannon. (n.d.). Midlands Ireland. https://www.midlandsireland.ie/places/river-shannon

Rock Of Dunamase. (n.d.-a). Discover Ireland. https://www.discoverireland.ie/laois/rock-of-dunamase

Rock of Dunamase. (n.d.-b). Laois Directory. https://laoistourism.ie/directory/list/things-to-do-in-laois-explore-irelands-ancient-east/key-attractions-in-laois-mountains-castles-adventure/rock-of-dunamase

Rock of Dunamase. (n.d.-c). Midlands Ireland. https://www.midlandsireland.ie/places/rock-of-dunamase

Roller, S. (n.d.). Mizen Head. History Hit. https://www.historyhit.com/locations/mizen-head

Roller, S. (2021a, February 18). Blarney Castle. History Hit. https://www.historyhit.com/locations/blarney-castle-2

Roller, S. (2021b, April 23). Titanic Belfast. History Hit. https://www.historyhit.com/locations/titanic-belfast

Roscommon. (n.d.). Discover Ireland. https://www.discoverireland.ie/roscommon/things-to-do

Roundwood House country accommodation in the midlands of Ireland. (n.d.). Roundwood House. https://roundwoodhouse.com

Royal Hibernian Academy. (n.d.). Visit Dublin. https://www.visitdublin.com/royal-hibernian-academy

Saint Colman's Cathedral. (n.d.). Discover Ireland. https://www.discoverireland.ie/cork/saint-colman-s-cathedral

Sea Mist House B&B. (n.d.). Sea Mist House. https://www.seamisthouse.com

Sean's Bar History. (n.d.). SeansBar.ie. https://www.seansbar.ie/seans-bar-history

17th century city walls. (n.d.). Discover Northern Ireland. https://discovernorthernireland.com/things-to-do/17th-century-city-walls-p685431

Shamrock Lodge Hotel. (n.d.). Tripadvisor. https://www.tripadvisor.ie/Hotel_Review-g212091-d601193-Reviews-Shamrock_Lodge_Hotel-Athlone_County_Westmeath.html

Sheeran, E. (2017). Galway girl [Streamed]. Atlantic Recording Corporation.

Slea Head Drive. (n.d.). Wild Atlantic Way. https://www.thewildatlanticway.com/sight/slea-head-drive

Slieve Bloom. (n.d.). Midlands Ireland. https://www.midlandsireland.ie/places/slieve-bloom

Slieve Bloom Mountain bike trails. (n.d.). Slieve Bloom. https://slievebloom.ie/biking/mountain-biking

Sligo. (n.d.). Discover Ireland. https://www.discoverireland.ie/sligo/things-to-do

6 incredible things to do in the Slieve Bloom Mountains. (n.d.). Discover Ireland. https://www.discoverireland.ie/offaly/things-to-do-slieve-bloom-mountains

Spielberg, S. (Director). (1993). Schindler's list [Film]. Universal Pictures.

SS Nomadic. (n.d.). Visit Belfast. https://visitbelfast.com/partners/ss-nomadic

St George's Market. (n.d.). Visit Belfast. https://visitbelfast.com/partners/st-georges-market

St Stephen's Green Park. (n.d.). OPW. https://www.ststephensgreenpark.ie

Star Wars in Ireland. (n.d.). Ireland. https://www.ireland.com/en-us/things-to-do/themes/ireland-on-screen/star-wars-in-ireland

Stay. (n.d.). Titanic Quarter. https://titanicquarter.com/stay/staying

Stormont Estate. (n.d.). Discover Northern Ireland. https://discovernorthernireland.com/things-to-do/stormont-estate-p715861

Story of the Fanad Lighthouse. (n.d.). Fanad Lighthouse. https://fanadlighthouse.com/our-story

Tacumshane Windmill. (n.d.). Discover Ireland. https://www.discoverireland.ie/wexford/tacumshane-windmill

Tain Way. (n.d.). Sport Ireland. https://www.sportireland.ie/outdoors/walking/trails/tain-way

10 basic phrases in the Irish language (Gaeilge). (n.d.). Gaelscoil Online. https://www.gaelscoilonline.com/blog/basicirishphrases

10 things you have to do in Ireland in the fall. (2021, May 13). Ireland. https://www.ireland.com/en-us/magazine/culture/ten-things-you-must-do-in-ireland-in-autumn

The 10 best things to do in Cavan. (n.d.). Discover Ireland. https://www.discoverireland.ie/cavan/best-things-to-do-cavan

The 11 best things to do in County Laois. (n.d.). Discover Ireland. https://www.discoverireland.ie/laois/things-to-do-laois

The Arthouse Library & Gallery. (n.d.). Laois Directory. https://laoistourism.ie/directory/list/things-to-do-in-laois-explore-irelands-ancient-east/the-arts-and-art-houses-and-galleries-in-co-laois/the-arthouse-library-gallery

The Blarney Castle. (n.d.). Blarney Castle & Gardens. https://blarneycastle.ie/blarney-castle

The Book of Kells. (n.d.). Visit Dublin. https://www.visitdublin.com/the-book-of-kells
The Brazen Head. (n.d.). Visit Dublin. https://www.visitdublin.com/the-brazen-head
The Burren. (n.d.). Cliffs of Moher. https://www.cliffsofmoher.ie/your-visit/beyond-the-cliffs-places-to-see/the-burren
The Dark Hedges. (n.d.). Discover Northern Ireland. https://discovernorthernireland.com/things-to-do/the-dark-hedges-p703291
The Dingle Peninsula. (n.d.). Ireland. https://www.ireland.com/en-ca/destinations/regions/dingle-peninsula/?ds_c=TI_CA_EN_PRO_PM_All+Island_NA_IOI_NA_NA_NA_ACP_Icons&ds_ag=Icons%7C Dingle+Peninsula&ds_k=things+to+do+in+dingle&gad_source=1&gclid=CjoKCQiApOyqBhDlARIsAGfnyM rdoSYlYRuTwm4I4vrF_k2VT6_zDkSupqtZseyj6HdGc-XPAqTVpdsaAo1iEALw_wcB&gclsrc=aw.ds
The Dock Arts Centre. (n.d.). Discover Ireland. https://www.discoverireland.ie/leitrim/the-dock-arts-centre
The English Market. (n.d.). English Market Cork. https://www.corkcity.ie/en/english-market
The Gobbins Cliff Path. (n.d.). Discover Northern Ireland. https://discovernorthernireland.com/things-to-do/the-gobbins-cliff-path-p710801
The Keadeen Hotel. (n.d.). Tripadvisor. https://www.tripadvisor.ie/Hotel_Review-g315876-d543199-Reviews-The_Keadeen_Hotel-Newbridge_County_Kildare.html
The River Shannon – Ireland's longest and most famous waterway. (n.d.). European Waterways. https://www.europeanwaterways.com/blog/river-shannon-irish-destination
The scenic beauty and charm of Westport. (n.d.). Ireland Travel Guide. https://www.myirelandtour.com/travelguide/our-travel/westport-weekend.php
The school years. (n.d.). Kylemore Abbey. https://www.kylemoreabbey.com/history/kylemore-abbey-school
The Táin Way. (n.d.). Carlingford and the Cooley Peninsula. http://carlingfordandcooleypeninsula.ie/carlingford-activities/walking-trails/t%C3%A1in-way
Things to do. (n.d.). National Parks of Ireland. https://www.nationalparks.ie/glenveagh/things-to-do
Tickets. (n.d.). Nano Nagle Place. https://maximcloud.co.uk/nanonagle/tickets
Tickets and tours. (n.d.). EPIC the Irish Emigration Museum. https://epicchq.com/visit/tickets-and-tours
Tollymore Forest Park. (n.d.). Nidirect. https://www.nidirect.gov.uk/articles/tollymore-forest-park
Tollymore Forest Park. (n.d.). Discover Northern Ireland. https://discovernorthernireland.com/things-to-do/tollymore-forest-park-p675461
Top 5 best things to do in Connemara National Park. (2023, October 23). Ireland before You Die. https://www.irelandbeforeyoudie.com/top-5-best-things-to-do-in-connemara-national-park
Top 7 reasons why you should visit Ireland-explore the world. (n.d.). SWAP. https://swap.ca/top-7-reasons-why-you-should-visit-ireland
Top things to do in Ireland in spring. (2022, January 6). Ireland. https://www.ireland.com/en-us/magazine/adventure-activities/top-things-to-do-spring
Tour prices. (n.d.). Bogside History Tours. https://bogsidehistorytours.com
Tower Tour. (n.d.). Fanad Lighthouse. https://fanadlighthouse.com/book-tower-tour/#book
Tucker, A. (Director). (2010). Leap year [Film]. Universal Pictures.
Uncover a True Hidden Gem in County Leitrim. (n.d.). Discover Ireland. https://www.discoverireland.ie/leitrim/things-to-do
Uncover Ireland's Ancient East. (n.d.). Discover Ireland. https://www.discoverireland.ie/irelands-ancient-east
Victoria Park. (n.d.). Visit Belfast. https://visitbelfast.com/partners/victoria-park
Visit Dunmore Head. (n.d.). Go to Ireland.com. https://www.go-to-ireland.com/what-to-see/dunmore-head
Visit the Mussenden Temple. (n.d.). Go to Ireland.com. https://www.go-to-ireland.com/what-to-see/the-mussenden-temple
Visit the Ulster Museum. (n.d.). Ulster Museum. https://www.ulstermuseum.org/visit
Visit us. (n.d.). Cork City Gaol. https://corkcitygaol.com/visit-us
Visitor information. (n.d.). Dún Eilíse Elizabeth Fort. https://www.corkcity.ie/en/elizabeth-fort/visitor-information
Walk the Walls – ramparts top and dry moat. (2014, July 17). The Derry Walls. https://thederrywalls.com/explore-the-walls
Wandering Jana. (n.d.). 8 recommendations for visiting historical sites. https://wanderingjana.com/2017/06/01/8-recommendations-for-visiting-historical-sites
Welcome to a world of contrast. (n.d.). Belvedere House. https://belvedere-house.ie
Welcome to Barberstown Castle Hotel. (n.d.). Barberstown Castle Hotel. https://www.barberstowncastle.ie
Welcome to Bramble Rock. (n.d.). Bramble Rock B&B. https://www.bramblerock.com/
Welcome to Doolin Cave. (n.d.). Doolin Cave. https://doolincave.ie
Welcome to Drimnagh Castle. (n.d.). Drimnagh Castle. https://www.drimnaghcastle.org
Welcome to Mallmore Country House. (n.d.). Mallmore Country House. https://www.mallmore.com/
Welcome to Otterstown House. (n.d.). Otterstown House Bed & Breakfast. Retrieved November 23, 2023, from https://otterstownhouse.com
Welcome to Scholars Townhouse Hotel. (n.d.). Scholars Townhouse Hotel. https://www.scholarshotel.com
Welcome to St Colmans Cathedral. (2020, March 30). St Colmans Cathedral. https://cobhcathedralparish.ie
Welcome to the Glenview Hotel and Leisure Club. (n.d.). Glenview Hotel and Leisure Club. https://www.glenviewhotel.com
Wesbrooks, E. (2015, March 2). What not to do in Dublin. Condé Nast Traveler. https://www.cntraveler.com/galleries/2015-03-02/what-not-to-do-in-dublin-ireland-city-guide
Wexford. (n.d.). Discover Ireland. https://www.discoverireland.ie/wexford/things-to-do?gad_source=1&gclid=CjoKCQjwy4KqBhDoARIsAEbCt6hV3T4dfjLS6xVZXy_kjsKHqGc47Z2vybkxOHG kzk2r6XPX42tbuzYaAlIAEALw_wcB
What to pack. (n.d.). Nordic Visitor Ireland. https://ireland.nordicvisitor.com/travel-guide/information/what-to-bring-pack
Where to stay in Belfast: Belfast's best neighborhoods. (2022, June 2). Wandertooth. https://www.wandertooth.com/where-to-stay-in-belfast-coolest-neighborhoods
Whitney, B. (n.d.). Liam Neeson. In Encyclopedia Britannica. https://www.britannica.com/biography/Liam-Neeson
Wicklow. (n.d.). Discover Ireland. https://www.discoverireland.ie/wicklow/things-to-do

Wolters World. (2021). Belfast: the don'ts of visiting Belfast, Northern Ireland [YouTube Video]. In YouTube. https://youtu.be/s_VjPz0OWvU?si=fWwaH1ruulLXAXRn
Youghal Clock Gate Tower. (n.d.). Discover Ireland. https://www.discoverireland.ie/cork/youghal-clock-gate-tower
Youghal Clock Gate Tower. (n.d.-b). Living Youghal. https://livingyoughal.ie/youghal-clock-gate-tower/overview/?_gl=1
Your glamping adventure in Ireland starts here. (n.d.). Glamping under the Stars. https://www.glampingunderthestars.ie
Zoological Museum. (n.d.). Visit Dublin. https://www.visitdublin.com/zoological-museum
Zoology. (n.d.). Trinity College Dublin. https://www.tcd.ie/Zoology

Image References

Anasch, R. (2018). Brown wooden barrel rack [Image]. Unsplash. https://unsplash.com/photos/brown-wooden-barrel-rack-HcaoLq2HGnw
Aziz, Y. (2018). Grayscale photo of building [Image]. Unsplash. https://unsplash.com/photos/grayscale-photo-of-building-fu1T1glXxGM
Beck, T. (2018). Black steel fence [Image]. In Unsplash. https://unsplash.com/photos/black-steel-fence-xhnimDJm0CU
Bond, T. (2022). Clonmacnoise is a ruined monastery situated in County Offaly in Ireland on the River Shannon south of Athlone, founded in 544 by Saint Ciarán, a young man from Rathcroghan, County Roscommon. [Image]. In Unsplash.
Craveiro, H. (2018). The Cliffs of Moher [Image]. Unsplash. https://unsplash.com/photos/rock-formation-beside-sea-under-white-sky-ezJhm4xrHAM
Cullen, B. (2016). Hook Lighthouse [Image]. Unsplash. https://unsplash.com/photos/white-and-red-concrete-lighthouse-7DS9AKLs23o
Fecker, L. (2020). Castle in Dublin [Image]. Unsplash. https://unsplash.com/photos/brown-concrete-building-under-blue-sky-during-daytime-W0sgNvhuQrg
Hindle, M. (2023). A view of the inside of a church looking up at the ceiling [Image]. Unsplash. https://unsplash.com/photos/a-view-of-the-inside-of-a-church-looking-up-at-the-ceiling-72QwC3c70KA
Hutchinson, I. (2022). The Baltimore Beacon in Cork [Image]. Unsplash. https://unsplash.com/photos/a-tall-white-tower-on-a-hill-by-the-ocean-ZJZZ5s0_eys
K. Mitch Hodge. (2019). Brown concrete building under blue sky during daytime [Image]. Unsplash. https://unsplash.com/photos/brown-concrete-building-under-blue-sky-during-daytime-cHTK1_sce0M
K. Mitch Hodge. (2021). Three Belfast landmarks in one shot. From left to right: Titanic Belfast, a museum for all things Titanic related; the very large Harland and Wolffe ship building crane Goliath; and immediately below it, the red bricked building where the Titanic was designed by Harland and Wolff prior to its fateful end in 1912 (May, 2019). [Image]. Unsplash. https://unsplash.com/photos/red-and-white-boat-on-water-near-green-and-white-building-during-daytime-OdQuwJulLLU
Kirwan, S. (2020). Person sitting on the edge of pyramid during sunset [Image]. Unsplash. https://unsplash.com/photos/person-sitting-on-the-edge-of-pyramid-during-sunset-C5tSgjZnU4o
Luddy, C. (2021). Sunrise at Fanad Lighthouse in Donegal, Ireland [Image]. Unsplash. https://unsplash.com/photos/a-lighthouse-on-a-rocky-shore-with-waves-crashing-in-front-of-it-vuCUMpCPXZU
Murphy, J. (n.d.). Cobh Co. Cork Ireland https://www.instagram.com/jaypix_01/ [Image]. Unsplash. https://unsplash.com/photos/white-and-black-concrete-building-under-blue-sky-during-daytime-rTG1TR6Ygbo
Steele, S. (2021). Classic architectural library on the edge of a cliff overlooking the coastal beach at dusk [Image]. In Unsplash. https://unsplash.com/photos/a-tower-on-the-side-of-a-cliff-next-to-a-body-of-water-bU-jSML_Vfc
ter Horst, L. (2022). Killarney National Park [Image]. Unsplash. https://unsplash.com/photos/a-body-of-water-with-trees-and-hills-in-the-background-X-U1_iauK2A
uncutURBEX. (2019). Kylemore Abbey [Image]. Pixabay. https://pixabay.com/photos/kylemore-abbey-ireland-castle-4152831/
Vella, J. (2023). Blarney Castle [Image]. Unsplash. https://unsplash.com/photos/a-view-of-a-castle-through-a-magnifying-glass-WAu-0ub8_RM
Walker, A. (2021). Shimna River [Image]. Unsplash. https://unsplash.com/photos/a-stone-bridge-over-a-river-surrounded-by-trees-8RpoZmZN1T8
Wilson, G. (2021). The Dark Hedges are a row of moody beech trees along a road in Northern Ireland. [Image]. Unsplash. https://unsplash.com/photos/a-road-lined-with-trees-on-both-sides-of-it-Oo8dpvYdhRk

Made in the USA
Coppell, TX
30 July 2024

35320691R00105